SURVIVING
&
THRIVING SOLO

To: VLADESCU

SURVIVING
& THRIVING SOLO
Options When You Live Alone

Frances Frommer

From: YOUR SECRET ADMIRER

authorHOUSE®

AuthorHouse™
1663 Liberty Drive
Bloomington, IN 47403
www.authorhouse.com
Phone: 1-800-839-8640

First published by AuthorHouse 9/11/2009

ISBN: 978-1-4490-2595-3 (sc)
ISBN: 978-1-4490-2594-6 (e)

Library of Congress Control Number: 2009909211

Printed in the United States of America
Bloomington, Indiana

This book is printed on acid-free paper.

Acknowledgments

I wish to thank all of the people listed below for their support and assistance in helping me to create this book.

Jo-an Collins, my writing teacher and friend, helped me to find my voice and read countless drafts as the book progressed.

I am most grateful to Jack Livesley, facilitator of Jolly Lits, my writing critique group, and all the members who encouraged and evaluated my work every step of the way. They are: Carole Barrett; Nancy Donnaperna; Robert Jones; Trish Kerr; Deb Lougheed; Barb MacDonald; Corinne McCorkle; Claire Moran; Barb Nobel; Marianne Pelletier; Isobel Raven; Bill Rundle; John M. Sargent; Joan Strathdee; Mickey Turnbull; Cathy Vance; and Gerda Voss. I couldn't have done it without you gals and guys.

Lina Jakusik, Elizabeth Mckay and Barbara Jaeger are friends who were always there for me with encouragement to keep writing and praise for my work.

Carol and Aileen Collinson and Aileen Landau are neighbors and friends who always offered praise and enthusiasm for my writing and illustrations.

Joanne Pedicone, librarian at Hamilton Public Library, always appreciated and published my book reviews in the staff newsletter.

Paul Lisson, librarian at Hamilton Public Library and a fellow writer who shared both difficult and joyous moments when my motivation needed a jolt.

Johnny Zhou of Canatel Computers in Mississauga repaired and maintained my computer, an essential tool in the writing process.

I am grateful to Shouvik Chowdhury for his computer expertise as he helped me to format my manuscript.

The members of Lakeview Toastmasters gave me the opportunity to develop my communication skills and find new friends.

I am grateful to Bev Tang-Kong, artist and community co-ordinator with Imagemaker Art Prints Studio in Mississauga, where I took classes in writing and art.

Ingrid Raudsepp gave me private yoga and pilates lessons so I could keep up my strength and stamina. Lanee Brown gave wonderful yoga classes where I learned to relax and rest my tired hands, wrists, neck and shoulders.

My brother, Sheldon, and sister-in-law, Annette, treated me to dinners and movies—most welcome entertainment and social contact.

A special thanks to Rosa Wang, graphic designer and owner of Graphic House, for her supportive enthusiasm and commitment to my book and her creative expertise in designing the layout of *Surviving & Thriving Solo.*

I thank Helena Quinton who provided luscious refreshments for my book launch.

My feline muses—Mooney (gone to heaven), Angel, and Star, provided constant companionship during the solitary hours.

FOREWORD

I never lived alone until I was in mid-life. Married at 18 straight from home, I lurched from marriage to marriage for years after that union failed. There were, of course, a variety of reasons for this but it was a time when all women were indoctrinated to believe she wasn't complete—or acceptable—without a male partner. After all, years ago, a woman alone was very suspect according to societal rules. The entire system was geared against her as a single entity and it made it very difficult to actually choose the path of being solo. As a result, few women willingly chose the single life. They sincerely believed being alone meant being lonely. They were sure it also meant ostracization, unhappiness and being unfulfilled.

Yet when I finally did become single and lived alone for the first time, I was astonished to find it was very different from what I had been led to believe. Far from being a time of unhappiness, I found it was very rewarding and satisfying in a multitude of ways. I discovered being alone did not have to mean being lonely but actually gave me space and room to develop emotionally and spiritually. And, far from being unfulfilled, it meant expanding my horizons in directions I could never have gone if I had been still willing to embrace the familiar constraints and compromise of a marital relationship.

By that time, society had (mostly) learned that a single woman was not a threat, an oddity or an object of pity to be shunned. She was finally seen as a viable and acceptable force of modern life.

Most beneficial of all, I discovered it opened a door into two wonderful worlds I had never experienced before—that of freedom and choice. That isn't to say there aren't moments of fear, doubt and anxiety in the solo life. I found those too and certainly when they have occurred, it would have helped enormously if such an enlightening and encouraging guide as *Surviving & Thriving Solo* by Frances Frommer had been available.

Here's an author who has not only explored every aspect of being in the single state but has embraced it with enthusiasm, common-sense and a rare clarity of mind. She makes it, in fact, a very special, even enviable, place to be. Her book shows that being single can be a wonderful opportunity to explore the meaning of self with confidence and optimism, going beyond the fears and doubts in order to reach out for a life in which anyone can flourish and be truly fulfilled.

She cheerfully embraces her single life, and in particular her pets, (advice I strongly endorse), and, in an instructional and brightly illustrated way, turns the tables on those who think the solo life is a colourless void. *Surviving & Thriving Solo* gives help, hope, laughter and an oft-needed boost of self esteem to the increasing numbers of people who are alone by life happenstance or who have chosen singledom as where they want to be—and stay.

Valerie Gibson

Valerie Gibson is the author of the best-selling book, "Cougar", about older women dating younger men. She is a well-known newspaper journalist, sex and relationship expert and radio and television personality in both Canada and the United States. Recent television appearances include American shows such as Dr. Phil, PrimeTime Live, CNBC's The Big Idea, Montel Williams and Maury, Entertainment Tonight and Canadian shows on CBC, Global, CTV, CITYTV and Rogers.

CONTENTS

PART 1 INTRODUCTION

My mother always told me that marriage was stepping from the frying pan into the fire. She intended this advice as a warning. To me, her words were a promise of a relationship full of romance, excitement and warmth. During my twenties, thirties and forties, I was driven by the dream of finding my perfect soul mate. I saw myself sitting in a garden in front of a beautiful house, surrounded by a husband, children, a dog and a cat and living happily ever after. However, my chosen partners were unable or unwilling to commit to marital bliss. When I turned fifty, I was still living alone. Nevertheless, over the years, I discovered how to survive AND thrive.

I stayed at home in the safety of my family with two parents, two younger brothers and two felines until I was 24 years old. Then, I moved into a duplex with three women for a year before I tackled my first apartment. It was like sliding around on a floor coated with baby oil as I took tiny steps to care for my home. Gradually, I put on rubber boots, got out my mop and cleaned the floor of my life. I tackled basic areas like work, relationships and interests, clearing negative thoughts and behaviors.

I have digested the statistics of the latest census. About one quarter of adults in both the United States and Canada live alone. I know that I am a member of the fastest growing type of household. I have made peace with the ups and downs. My journey was not all fun and games.

On the one hand, I have experienced great angst. This was most marked when I was without a man in my younger years. After every relationship ended, intense anxiety overwhelmed me. Evenings after work, weekends and vacations also created stress in my life. I had to find answers to many questions. Could I afford to take the day off work to contact the government by telephone? What would I tackle first when I had the flu, the cat was howling, the car was in the garage and my veterinarian's office was closed? What could I do when alone during a power blackout and the batteries of my flashlight were dead and I had no candles? Was it better to go to a dance or surf the Internet for my next date? What could I do when the saran wrap would not unwrap and I was out of tin foil?

On the other hand, I have known wondrous ecstasy while living alone. I felt powerful as I mastered basic chores. I filled my free time at home alone with creative activities such as painting and writing, meditation and self-love. I was blessed with a great career as a librarian and had access to zillions of self-help and humor books to lift my spirit. I linked with other people such as single, divorced and widowed women, in support groups and at other activities. I got a computer with Internet. If lonely at midnight, I was able to chat with friends around the world by e-mail. Adding the comfort of cats to my home created constant delight.

I began to focus upon how to add pleasure and fun to my life. Would I spend a whole weekend writing my book? Could I stay up all night watching Woody Allen movies in bed while eating pizza? Should I do my housework only every other month (except for cleaning

the floors for the felines)? Would I paint my living room red
or purple?

Surviving & Thriving Solo is a book that wrote me. After a series of
losses, I found the light at the bottom of my shopping bag by writing about my options. I recorded my experiences and desperately
searched for alternatives in my relationships, home and work areas.
At first, I felt like a dot in a box—powerless and helpless. Gradually,
I grabbed my angst by the feet, ankles and belly button. I learned
how to transform black and gray states of mind into a dazzling rainbow of colors.

My life became bright and full of fun most of the time. My hours
alone at home were treasures that I valued. New activities and relationships burst through the clouds. Ladies and gentlemen of all ages,
I share my journey with you in order to inform, amuse, entertain
and guide your journeys through the ups and downs of living alone.

This book is guaranteed to help you examine your choices as a
person who lives alone. You may be single, divorced, widowed or
separated. Surviving & Thriving Solo is intended to add lightness and
brightness to your life by:

❀   Discussing experiences and concerns we share as people who
live alone;

❀   Presenting you with a variety of options in basic life areas in
the form of checklists;

❀   Entertaining you by expressing choices that range from the
absurd to the practical, illustrated with cartoon drawings;

❀   Inspiring you to appreciate the opportunities and challenges
that are available to you;

❀   Providing you with an annotated reading list of books that
I found stimulating in my quest for a satisfying life.

PART 2

ON BEING
AT HOME ALONE

Bloom where you're planted. This is the message on a treasured
greeting card on my mirror. It took me many years to surrender to
the fact that I was living alone. I was a lady-in-waiting for my prince.
I dreaded going home. I resisted decorating. I did not learn how to
cook for myself. I escaped from my feelings of loneliness by indulging
in overeating. Self-pity over lack of a partner often overwhelmed me.
Gradually, I identified with the caterpillar that becomes a chrysalis
and then a powerful yet delicate butterfly. My life began to bloom.

I faced my 14 walls. I filled them with prints of the sea, sunflowers
by Van Gogh and scenes of Tahiti by Gaugin. Plants were placed
in every room. I bought white lacquered furniture that I adored.

Curtains and pillows in greens, blues, yellows and pinks added relaxing and cheerful colors to my haven.

I learned to love my own company. Loneliness was transformed into solitude. My time alone became an opportunity to meditate, to explore my spirituality and to develop my inner strength. My commitments to painting and writing ensured that I was never alone without enjoyable and meaningful activities.

I knew that I could connect to the outside world by telephone, television, radio and the computer. Self-help books filled my bookshelves. There was a wealth of information to guide me in nourishing my body and soul, fixing mood disorders and cutting toenails.

In addition, Mooney entered my life. He was a blue point Siamese with intense turquoise eyes like the blue waters of the Caribbean. It was a joy to stroke his sleek fur, softer than velvet or silk. He had the disposition of an angel, overflowing with continuous unconditional love. Mooney was my constant companion when I was alone at home and coping with changes in relationships, apartments or jobs. He was a delightful playmate and we had great fun with mice, bells and balls. My progress as a survivor who was thriving came to a halt in February of 1999. When Mooney was almost seventeen, he died of kidney failure. I experienced one of the worst and most painful times of my life. When I left the veterinarian's office and entered my apartment, an avalanche of grief washed over me. With the help of members of a pet loss support group, I gradually recovered. It was healing to share sad feelings and learn ways to cope like writing in a journal and remembering happy times. Although Mooney's paw prints are stuck in my heart, I was able to bring two more felines into my life almost a year later. My hearth was full of purring, playing and cuddling again. I was able to return to my skills of being alone at home and go on with my life.

1. LEAVING WORK

 Even though I eventually had a cat in my life, I avoided leaving work until the last moment. I was anxious because there wouldn't be anyone to greet me when I arrived home. I often worked late. I arranged to go for coffee, a drink or a meal with colleagues to pass a few hours. Shopping and strolling around a mall were also favorite activities. Browsing in a bookstore in the section on self-help books gave me strength. I signed up for evening classes. Since there would not be enough time to go home first, I could eat in a restaurant and have some dinner conversation with the waiter or waitress.

Sooner or later I knew that I had to go home. I envied my co-workers who would rush home to their spouses and children. Then I realized that most of them had to face another job of cooking a meal for others, doing housework and caring for demanding children. I could stroll to my car at a leisurely pace. There was time to enjoy the warm sunshine on my face or to gaze at the twinkling lights of starry skies. I began to look forward to the fact that I could do whatever I fancied when I arrived home. However, I had to do the following: recover from my day of labor, bathe and wash off the dust from the library, cook a quick meal such as boiling a few eggs and making toast, clean the dishes or leave them to soak until the weekend, relax with television or a book, have a few moments for a hobby like knitting, and prepare my clothes and a lunch for the next day of work. Other than these tasks, my time was my own. Over the years, I learned that there are many options to add enjoyment to your trip home from work.

So, Can You, Should You, Might You or Will You?!?!

Checklist of Choices

☐ Be grateful that you have earned some disability insurance and pension for your golden years. You may be your only caretaker.

☐ Focus on the thought that all of your pay belongs just to you. Buy a new suede couch to help you to enjoy your evenings alone.

☐ Have a cassette or CD in your car ready to entertain you as you travel. Wear earphones if you are walking or using public transit. Choose Woody Allen telling jokes, not funeral marches.

- [ ] Fill your mind with positive thoughts such as a day without a headache. If you have one when you leave work, no one will prevent you from spending the evening under the covers with Tylenol.

- [ ] Decorate your entrance hall so you will rejoice upon entering your home. Hang bells from the ceiling and pictures of clowns waving at you on the walls.

- [ ] Consider a cuddly pet such as a cat or dog or buy a teddy bear. If you choose a live creature (or two), you will have a constant little prisoner of love to welcome you home.

- [ ] Pick up your mail daily to feel wanted and needed, if only by MasterCard, Visa and American Express. Pen pals, magazine subscriptions and donations to charities can also give you regular mail.

- [ ] Call your friends to feel a sense of connection and social support. When you are on your own, there is no competition for the phone and no one telling you to make your call short.

- [ ] Prepare a bubble bath and sink into a blissful state of serenity, pleasure and sensual ecstasy. Add a rose-scented candle and some harp or flute music. Throw in bath salts for sore muscles. The cares of the day will float away.

2. DOING DINNER FOR ONE

Dining alone at home or in a restaurant is a challenge. Cutting up vegetables for a salad and cooking some chicken or fish can feel like an exhausting task after a day of work. It is easy to avoid preparing an interesting and healthy meal just for myself. Heating up frozen dinners and ordering food from a restaurant is so convenient. I confess to sometimes eating from a pot or drinking directly from a carton when I am tired.

I gradually came to believe that I deserved a tasty and nourishing meal, especially on weekends when I could spend more time in the kitchen. I have discovered that there are many wonderful cookbooks written for the person who is cooking for one. My whole dinner might not be as plentiful or tasty as the food at a Jewish bar-mitzvah or Italian wedding. But, sometimes, it is worth the effort required to prepare some fried shrimps with wild rice, a spinach salad and chocolate cheesecake. Adding a few candles, soft music and a glass of sparkling wine can definitely lift my spirits.

Dining out alone is always an option when I crave a great meal but prefer not to shop or cook. However, I know that it is necessary to brace myself for some moments of tension that can occur when I enter a restaurant on my own. When asked "how many?," I say "one" with a pleasant smile. I focus on the word "fun" or any other rhyming word such as "gun" in order to stifle a silent scream. It seems obvious to me that I am standing alone.

If I am placed in the center of a restaurant, surrounded by couples and families, I firmly request a table in the corner where I can slide onto the floor when necessary. I keep a list of dining establishments that have cozy corners and booths. I watch for places that attract solitary diners such as airports, bus terminals and train stations. I carry books and newspapers to amuse myself after I have finished reading the menu ten times. I know that I can also sit and plan to bring a friend with me the next time I go out to dinner. Since you are likely to crave dinner at least seven times a week, it is wise to cultivate your cooking skills and find ways to enjoy dining alone.

So, Can You, Should You, Might You or Will You?!?!

Checklist of Choices

☐ When dining alone at home, enjoy the fact that you can dress any old way. A t-shirt or velour housecoat is acceptable. Lying naked on your side can also be comfortable.

☐ Dine whenever you like. Choose six o'clock, eight o'clock or midnight. You can do whatever you like. Your clocks belong to you.

☐ Eat whatever you fancy. A sandwich of bananas, peanut butter and ketchup is tasty. Add some potato chips. No one is around to criticize you for omitting a salad.

- [ ] Roast a chicken and bake a cake when you have the time and desire. You can use up some of that poultry seasoning and nutmeg in your cupboard.

- [ ] Let yourself order in pizza or Chinese food some of the time. You will have a four-minute date as you greet the delivery man to pay for your meal.

- [ ] Eat with plastic cutlery and paper plates. You can just throw away the dishes after your meal. Leave china plates and silver cutlery to be soaked and washed on the weekend.

- [ ] Entertain yourself with your television, radio, CD player or cassette recorder. You can also use your computer if you are good at typing and eating simultaneously.

- [ ] If you have pets, place their dishes near your table or couch where you dine. You can munch together and exchange winks.

- [ ] When dining out alone, carry a book, a newspaper, a cell phone or a laptop computer. You can only read the menu so many times.

- [ ] Appreciate your next steady relationship. Choose someone who will take you to restaurants and loves to cook, at their place.

3. BATTLING THE BULGE

After I learned how to create delicious meals for myself, I found that I was eating more. No one was watching me if I took second or seventh helpings of dinner rolls or donuts. Leftovers of lasagna were not always saved for the next day.

After awhile, when I gazed into the mirror, I was startled by the sight of a pear-shaped body rather than one that resembled an hour glass. My belly was bulging rather than flowing in a straight line. I read *The South Beach Diet* and *Dr. Atkins' New Diet Revolution* many times. I discovered that I was an emotional eater.

But, food often gave me sensual delight and reduced my angst while I was learning how to live alone. Eating would quickly banish moods of loneliness and anger and stop me from committing crimes of violence. I also ate more in company as my stomach expanded. Compared to a cigarette, tap water or a sweet sherry, eating is usually socially acceptable.

I believed the biblical message that for everything there is a season. I learned to be kind to myself and accepted a few extra bulges in all the wrong places from time to time. However, I never threw away my books and articles on dieting. I can begin to slim down again and again when I am ready.

So, Can You, Should You, Might You or Will You?!?!

Checklist of Choices

☐ Be grateful that you do not crave heroin or cocaine. The cost is at least double the price of a pizza with triple cheese, garlic and onions.

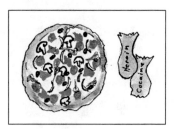

☐ Take a book and comfort food to bed with you. Bagels with cream cheese and cookies are good choices.

☐ Ladies, release the seams on your blouses and add stylish slits up the sides of vests. Gentlemen, you can buy a new belt with more notches.

- [ ] Think about how cuddly your plump cat, dog or teddy bear feels. There will be more of you to hug and love when you are pleasantly plump.

- [ ] Stock up your kitchen with lettuce, celery and carrots plus peanut butter, crackers, jam, cream cheese and ice-cream. You will have a choice when hunger strikes.

- [ ] Throw away your scale. You know that your doctor always has one in his office when you feel like dieting and weighing yourself.

- [ ] Type your list of the joys of being slim in large print and capital letters. For example, your clothes will fit and you can spend less on food. Running up the stairs without collapsing is also pleasant.

4. DEALING WITH THE BLUES

 I am happy in my home and with my life most of the time. Yet I know that the blues will strike on occasion, especially when I am at home alone for many hours. Loneliness and self-pity can surface and take over. It is as though a gray, dark blue or black cloud hangs over my head.

Since I have no one at home to comfort and uplift me on a regular basis, it is easy to sink into a blue mood when minor or major concerns surface. After I visit a happy couple or attend a shower or wedding, my mood can sink to quite a low level. I yearn for a mate. When I think about my finances I wonder if I will be able to pay my bills. Prices of goods and services rise while my income stays the same. Who will help me with the chores when I am sick? My cats don't make chicken soup. Who can I telephone at around midnight? My shrink is not on call after 9 p.m. in the evening.

I have found that it is important to accept the blues and plan for ways of dealing with them and their causes. When I have lost a friend, parent or pet to death, I knew that I had to cry, let myself grieve and then start to remember our happy times. Asking for social support from friends and family or groups is essential.

I get depressed when friends don't call for awhile. I have to decide whether or not to telephone them or find new ones who might be more attentive. When my cat throws up on fresh laundry, I get quite upset. I have to find my inner strong lady and just do another wash. When a relationship ends, I listen to my Billie Holiday and Leonard Cohen tapes with songs about love that has been desired and lost. When I start to miss all those old friends and lovers who were boring or emotionally abusive, I know that it is time to turn towards music rather than trying to begin again with people who have hurt me. Thank goodness I ripped up their photographs and threw out their home telephone numbers.

I can also look at cartoons and hope a smile will erupt. I keep a file with uplifting items such as inspiring quotations, pictures of beautiful scenery and favorite recipes. I create lists of things that I can do when a black and blue mood strikes like cleaning a closet, calling a good friend and counting my blessings. I strive to see the difference between what I can and cannot change. Some beams of light usually appear and I find my way towards more colorful experiences. Know that sunshine and rainbows appear regularly. However, don't throw away your umbrella and boots.

So, Can You, Should You, Might You or Will You?!?!

Checklist of Choices

☐ Open the curtains and soak in some sunlight. If it is raining, turn on a lamp. Light a few candles.

☐ Review your self-love exercises with the mirror. Look into your eyes and tell yourself what a wonderful and loveable person you are.

☐ Chat with your pet, if you have one. Even fish will move towards you if you drop flakes into the tank.

- [ ] Keep a journal. Scribble with black, blue, red and yellow crayons.

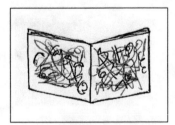

- [ ] Write affirmations. Consider: "I am strong; I am happy; I am glad there was not a tsunami in my neighborhood today."

- [ ] Be good to yourself and exercise. Even moving your head from side to side or strolling to another room can change your mood.

- [ ] Read the book *Fit For Life*. Have a snack of fresh fruit or fat-free yogurt. If this does not hit the spot, you might choose french fries with gravy and some hot chocolate if you decide to indulge.

- [ ] Join a group that gives you regular social contact. Share your grief, your habits of overeating or your love of a good poker game.

- [ ] List what you like in your life. Nothing is too small. Note the honey on your morning toast, a purr from your cat when you wake in the morning or piles of laundry that you can leave until next month.

- [ ] Dress for success to attract new people into your life and get away from your blue mood. Wear bright red clothing but stay away from bulls.

5. SHAPING SELF-HELP SKILLS

 Since I live on my own, I know that I alone am responsible for everything related to my survival. I must pay my bills in order to have shelter, food, transportation and kitty litter. Heat and electricity are also desirable. I have to keep in shape to take care of myself and my cats, Angel and Star. I also require some fun and entertainment. The occasional movie, lipstick and a new pair of shoes add spice to life. My passions for painting and writing require a few dollars. I need canvases, paint and brushes plus paper and cartridges for the computer printer.

I am pleased to live in this twenty-first century since there are so many media that offer self-help guidelines: books, videos, cassettes, compact discs, DVDs, electronic books, and Internet sites on the computer. Many of these sources tell us THE definitive solution to problems and include rules of behavior to give results that will last forever.

I maintain a library of books and articles related to survival skills like bending correctly, giving a cat a pill and fixing a blocked sink. I rush to buy anything with a title that begins with the words "The Joy of" or "The Secret of." I note, however, that electronic media require some electricity and they are not available during power failures due to winter storms, earthquakes or hurricanes. I can use these mediums when I am at home by myself and can proceed at my own rate with privacy. Thus, I am not always dependent upon other people or running out to a course.

Managing my mind can be a full-time obsession. I keep myself in mental shape by cultivating nine qualities. They are: strength, courage, compassion, patience, acceptance, gratitude, tolerance, imagination, and faith. Posting quotations and cartoons around my home keeps me on track when the blues strike or feelings of weakness start to surface. A favorite cartoon is Tom Wilson's Ziggy character showing him smiling and saying "The nice thing about being your own best friend…is that you're always around when you need you!!" I remind myself that I am not in training for the Olympics or preparing for childbirth. So, I also allow myself time off to relax and do nothing when the mood strikes. Even self-improvement and working on survival can be carried to extremes if we are constantly nagging ourselves.

So, Can You, Should You, Might You or Will You?!?!

Checklist of Choices

☐ Study the book *Awaken the Giant Within* by Anthony Robbins. See also the comics in your daily newspaper.

- Visualize yourself as a strong man or woman. Dress up like Superman or Catwoman. Bounce back like a ball after panic attacks or disappointing experiences.

- Pretend that you are the lion in the land of Oz. Believe that the Wizard will give you enough courage to get to the next singles' dance.

- Be good to yourself. When you crave human touch, go for a facial, pedicure and massage. Give yourself a daily hug.

- Be patient with yourself. You can move slowly in your own home. No one is waiting for the toothpaste, telephone or computer.

- Enjoy the fun you can have with your freedom. You can explore anything without interruption. Play solitaire all night or dance naked to erotic music.

- [ ] Appreciate every little accomplishment. Be grateful when you find a clean sweater. Washing a coffee mug and one pot can also be satisfying.

- [ ] Learn to be tolerant. Reach out to other people for the good and bad times. Ignore your neighbor's garlic breath if he is handy with a hammer and screwdriver.

- [ ] Use your imagination to remember past good times such as that cool glass of wine at a café in Paris. Look forward to having your dreams come true such as winning the lottery.

- [ ] Have faith in Spirit, angels or fairies as helpmates in times of need. Welcome any source that will help you to fix the sink. You can also call the plumber.

6. DISCOVERING YOUR CREATIVITY

Creativity can be defined as using your imagination to find totally new and innovative approaches to challenges. I discovered a passion for painting and writing. Spending my time in these two activities makes my time at home alone meaningful and full of joy. When I paint, time stands still. All problems and anxieties dissolve. I become energized and refreshed. I regularly create mandalas, pictures within a circular form. This is sacred art. I meditate, then create designs representing my spiritual journey, using many materials such as watercolors, markers, sparkles and stickers. I have exhibited several times and even sold a few paintings. Besides writing letters, to-do lists and filling out income tax returns, I write in a journal on a regular basis. This gives me a constant treasured companion to whom I can vent blue feelings or focus upon topics such as the joy of living alone or the pleasure of eating chocolate-chip cookies. My journal-writing has given birth to writing book reviews, articles and stories. Some have even been published.

There are many directions you can explore to find your passions. Would you like to write a short story about dating disasters, a poem about true love or a novel about the Civil War? You can also keep a journal to express your dreams, goals, nightmares and grocery lists.

Only you will see the content.

Might you like to paint pictures? Visit an art supply store and see oil, watercolor and acrylic paints in a full rainbow of colors and a wondrous assortment of brushes and papers or canvases. Colored and graphite pencils or charcoal might catch your fancy for sketching or creating drawings of the exquisite rooms in your new home. You don't need a studio and can work on the kitchen table if you live in a small space. Have you considered sculpting? You can purchase simple materials like play dough to create a figurine or coffee mug.

Are you happiest in the kitchen? Make some muffins and enjoy the sweet scents of vanilla and nutmeg. Looking at the colors of red tomatoes, yellow peppers and green zucchinis for a soup can banish a blue mood. If you are not experienced, there are lots of books and television shows that will show you how easy and creative cooking can be.

Would you enjoy collecting? Your mind will be occupied as you search for a special coin or figurine, research in books or on the internet, organize, label and display the objects of your choice.

Do you want to use your creativity to decorate and make your home into a fabulous retreat and haven? Choose soft pastel colors for your walls or wallpaper with a seascape theme, scenes of the ocean and palm trees. Add fountains, seashell mobiles, plants and whimsical objects like leather fish. Velvet and silk pillows in turquoise and emerald green scattered on your couch can soothe your senses and be a delight to stroke.

You have only yourself to please. If you are beginning with a blank mind, unsure of what might kindle the fire in your soul, start on a small scale. To discover your passions, read books, take a course or visit a store that sells art supplies. Go to a hobby show or browse in a furniture store. Take a walk in a park or by a lake. Gradually, you will discover what are the most meaningful ways for you to express your creativity.

So, Can You, Should You, Might You or Will You?!?!

Checklist of Choices

☐ Express yourself with colored pencils, markers or paints. Scribble like you did in kindergarten to contact your inner artist.

☐ Write a bit each day in a journal. If blocked, copy out the alphabet or the numbers from one to ten. Try Hebrew or Greek as you progress.

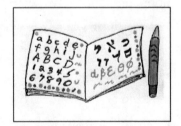

☐ Place your hands in a bowl of tapioca pudding to test your interest in sculpting. Move on to clay or marble when you are ready.

- Get out a hammer, nails and a few pieces of wood. Build bookshelves for your self-help books. A swizzle stick is also a good project.

- Be adventurous in the kitchen. Bake a sea bass with peanut butter sauce and brandy. Steam some fiddleheads. Add wild rice.

- Knit or crochet a scarf. If you prefer a smaller project, create a cover for your thimble or toaster.

- Collect postage stamps or Picasso prints. Buttons or quotations are good choices if your budget is limited.

- [ ] Decorate to express your wildest dreams. You might crave red walls with a purple carpet. Or create a serene Caribbean scene with fishnets and wallpaper with a seashell pattern.

- [ ] Join groups related to your interests. Take courses and attend workshops. You are free to try anything. UFO clubs? Snake breeder societies?

7. EXPERIENCING THE COMPANY OF A PET

 Who are the best lovers? For me, cats of course. Your choice might be a dog, a bird, a hamster or a fish. I lived entirely alone for many years before inviting an animal companion into my life. I learned to love my home, enjoy my own company and fill my time with meaningful activities. However, when Mooney, my first feline, entered my life, I didn't know how I had lived without him.

He was a Siamese cat who was a warm bundle of constant love and he adored me. Mooney would run to greet me as soon as I stepped into my apartment. Whenever I needed some love, purrs, hugs and cuddles, he was there for me. We had delightful play sessions with mice, pieces of tin foil and buttons. It was easy to surrender to being owned by him. Who else would sniff and lick my armpit before my shower after work?

After he passed away at the age of 17, two new cats entered my life. Angel is a gentle Russian Blue with sparkling green eyes and a smile that lights up the room. Star is a spunky Burmese who loves to cuddle and be held. Despite all of the fun and games, there are moments when my nerves get jangled. Star likes to talk at 2 a.m. when I am falling asleep or at 7 a.m. when I plan to sleep in. Angel sometimes throws up on fresh laundry. Both cats jump onto the table when I am entertaining. Although they are spotless from regular self-cleaning, most dinner guests prefer to have place mats free of cat hair.

Star has had coughing fits in the middle of the night in winter. Once, this occurred when the car wasn't working and I had the flu. My best friend who usually took me to the vet was out of town. At such moments, it is important to avoid pet abuse. I remember my commitment to care for my cats despite the hassles that occur from time to time. So, when your pet frustrates you, it is wise to recall the good times and precious moments.

So, Can You, Should You, Might You or Will You?!?!

Checklist of Choices

☐ Give your pets all the attention they deserve. Offer them tons of cuddles and a tin of their favorite food plus a dozen toys. You will also enjoy playtime.

☐ When mad at your pet, vent your true feelings openly and honestly. Use a gentle tone of voice and stroke his or her fur (or feathers).

☐ Do things together. Share your favorite music or meditation time. Relaxation is good for all your souls.

- [ ] If you feel like exploding after Fido chews your favorite shoe, board him or her at a kennel for a day. It is better to lose some money than your temper and your pet due to murder.

- [ ] Allow your pet to spend the evening on your lap. Your muscles might cramp but your blood pressure will go down and so will your medical and veterinarian bills.

- [ ] When anger threatens your relationship, immediately planseparate vacations. Time apart can allow you to cool down, improve your special bond and avoid disaster.

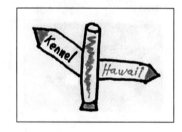

- [ ] Enjoy their warm presence at bedtime. Hope that they will sleep through the night, at least until the sun rises.

PART 3

ON TACKLING THE CHORES & OTHER BASICS

In order to enjoy my time at home alone, I must do a few chores. I classify my chores into indoor and outdoor tasks. I have reduced the number of indoor tasks by hiring a cleaning lady to come in once a month. What a blessing to return from work to sparkling floors, dust-free furniture and windows that present a clear view to the world outside. I am often afraid to use my stove, my sinks and my bathtub for a few days in case I banish the sparkling surfaces. I will eat take-out food so I don't dirty the oven and prefer a shower to avoid cleaning the bathtub. I strive to control clutter and my slothful habits for a week or two.

Each day, I still have to cook a bit, like making toast or hot cereal for breakfast. I also wash a few dishes, feed my cats and pick up my snail mail. Gradually, piles of clothes and papers build up. Dust appears on my furniture again. However, I know that I can always call the cleaning lady to visit me again before the month is up, for a price of course. Since there is no partner to help me, I feel I deserve this treat at least once a month. I can even squeeze in a bit of a social life on weekends since there are fewer chores on my list after the cleaning lady has left.

I have only two hands and two feet, usually weary after a week of work. So venturing outdoors for the rest of the chores can be a physical challenge. I always have my pension cheque deposited directly into the bank and use several credit cards to reduce visits to the teller. Yet, cash is necessary at times, like for a cup of coffee or a postage stamp. The car needs gas when the tank is empty. I must visit the drug store, cleaner's, shoemaker's and pet food store on a regular basis. A trip to the supermarket is essential unless I want to order in food every night. Few places deliver breakfast, cleaning supplies or snacks such as popcorn. In addition, I sometimes fancy a new housecoat or a pair of slippers and a bottle of wine and a video to entertain me during the evening when I am at home alone. A new car, computer or couch may be on my agenda. My solution to this list of tasks is to add a treat to my outing. It may be a cappuccino with a piece of chocolate cake at a café. Or, I browse at the pet store, play with the toys and buy a mouse with catnip for my cats. Strolling through a nursery for a bouquet of colorful and fragrant flowers or a new plant is also a delight after a journey from store to store. It is so energizing to browse among bouquets of fresh flowers such as tulips and daffodils in late winter. Strolling by palm trees reminds me of vacations in southern climates.

1. HANDLING HOUSEWORK

 Even though I sometimes have a cleaning lady, there is still a bit of housework left for me to do. Clutter grows as I cook, eat, bathe and relax. The cats leave their toys everywhere. However, I am free to clean when I choose. I can dust at midnight. I can pick up a few papers during a television commercial. I can leave dirty dishes soaking in the sink for several days. I can also set my own standards of cleanliness and tidiness. There is no one to impress or scold me if I leave my socks on the floor. I have total control over who enters and sees my home.

The one exception is the superintendent. When the sink overflows or the toilet is blocked, I must invite him over for a visit. If I am out and water is flowing into the apartment below me, he is also free to enter my apartment to do the necessary repairs. Unexpected emergencies usually happen when I am definitely not ready for company. I was recently quite embarrassed when I needed help with the pipes under the sink in my bathroom as water was dripping at a furious pace. My hall was full of shoes, boots and dust. Pantyhose and several pieces of lingerie hung over my bathtub. The litter box was screaming for a cleaning. I now keep air freshener in the hall and have places to hide my wet lingerie in a blue plastic bag behind the bathroom door. I control my panic and tidy a tiny bit before I make the phone call inviting the superintendent to come over immediately. Besides planning for both unexpected and invited visitors, I strive to streamline my housework chores and add a bit of fun to necessary tasks.

So, Can You, Should You, Might You or Will You?!?!

Checklist of Choices

☐ Use only one bowl, one cup, one set of cutlery and one plate. Rinse them after each use to avoid washing a load of dishes.

☐ Wear each outfit five times. You will have less laundry. Use a lot of perfume or after-shave before going out.

☐ Buy linens and clothing that do not require ironing. Do take suede and fur items to the cleaner's.

☐ Purchase a duster made of feathers. It can double as a toy for your dog or cat.

☐ Buy dusters and J-cloths in bright pink, turquoise and yellow. Wiping surfaces will become a colorful experience.

☐ Wash floors and vacuum carpets only when the cat starts to cough. Also do this when you see sticky substances and dust balls on the soles of your slippers.

☐ Buy only cactus plants or plastic flowers. Little or no water is required.

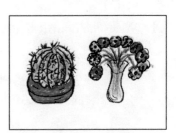

☐ Hang sun-catchers on your windows. You will not notice the dirt and can avoid washing the windows indefinitely.

- [ ] Leave your clothes lying around. Pick them up only when it is time to do the laundry.

- [ ] Let papers and mail pile up until the stacks topple over. Or, store them in a large carton and do not open until the weekend.

2. SHOPPING FOR ONE

"Only one piece of salmon?" When the lady at the fish counter stares at me in amazement, I am tempted to change my mind and ask for two pieces. However, I prefer my fish fresh and really don't want to eat salmon two days in a row. I also have to plan ahead when selecting fresh vegetables. Do I want to eat cauliflower or broccoli every night? At least I can select only a few handfuls of green beans, one red pepper or a single potato. Spices and sugar come in containers that will last me for at least a whole year. Thank goodness a loaf of bread or bag of bagels can be stored in the freezer.

Shopping for one has to be viewed as a creative challenge in which we have some power to reduce stress and self-consciousness. I go to the deli counter at the supermarket where it is okay to request two slices of turkey or cheese. Small containers are available for salads. I also look for bulk food stores or supermarkets where I can buy only two scoops of nuts or raisins rather than a large container suitable for 16 people. Shopping at a farmer's market can be fun. Browsing at the colorful and interesting displays and receiving personal service is a refreshing change from lining up at a large store. Also, their food is likely to be fresher than produce that has traveled from South America or Mexico.

I need to gather all of my muscular strength before I go out to do my shopping. In my twenties, I could carry six shopping bags of groceries for several blocks but those days are gone. I know that I can get everything I need in one trip to a large supermarket. However, they have gigantic and heavy shopping carts; the smaller ones are usually taken. When I shop for groceries, I usually also visit the pharmacy, pet food store and library. So, I have quite a few shopping bags. After visiting each place, I have to take my parcels from the stores to the car. At the end of my journey, I then have to carry everything from the car to the elevator to my apartment. I never leave home without my shopping cart. This does help and saves me from making ten trips to get my parcels into my home. I always hope that the cart will not tip over as I wheel it from my car to the elevator. I reward myself for the achievement of shopping with a generous portion of cashews or ice cream when I crash on the couch. I dream of a mall for singles where all stores deliver. There is also a doctor, dentist and café for connecting.

So, Can You, Should You, Might You or Will You?!?!

Checklist of Choices

☐ Plan ahead and buy only eight items at a time at the supermarket and qualify for the Express Exit. You might have to eat lightly and shop again.

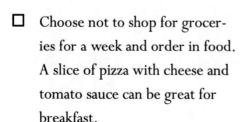

☐ Choose not to shop for groceries for a week and order in food. A slice of pizza with cheese and tomato sauce can be great for breakfast.

☐ Buy that large cabbage and huge bunch of carrots. You can enjoy coleslaw for lunch and dinner for the next 17 days.

- [ ] If you feel self-conscious among the families and couples, shop as if you are cooking for five. You will fit in with the crowd but might binge on large portions at home.

- [ ] Invite a friend or two along when you shop. They can carry the parcels. You can also ask the cashier if someone can help you to carry your groceries to the car.

- [ ] Find a drug store that delivers. You don't want to be without essentials like vitamin pills, toilet paper and potato chips.

- [ ] Purchase many items through the Internet like books, clothes, videos and vitamins. You will only have to go out once to get your packages from the post office.

- [ ] Appreciate the freedom that you have to select items that meet only your needs. You can buy croissants rather than whole wheat bread, rent five Woody Allen films and splurge on that red dress with matching shoes.

3. PAYING......SAFELY

As I do my shopping, I worry about carrying and exposing my money. If I have to make purchases by moonlight, my anxiety increases. I envy men who can keep their wallets in the pocket of their trousers or inside their jacket.

I often wonder about what style of purse is best? I look at those pouches you can wear around your hips. However, I am already bulky in that area and do not want to carry another few pounds below my waist. I consider using only a little change purse that I could keep in my bra. My friend never carries a purse or wallet but keeps everything in a tote bag, even loose coins and bills. I have settled for a shoulder bag that I wear around my neck and across my chest. My wallet is placed in a compartment with a zipper.

There are so many homeless people on the streets. I sometimes give them a bit of change and hope they will not follow me. When I go to the bank for cash, I drive home immediately. I trust that no burglars are watching me and recording my license plate number and the model of my car. I feel safest shopping in drug stores and supermarkets. They have large mirrors for security. I assume that the members of the staff are honest. Of course it is necessary to open my wallet at times and remove money to pay various small purchases like a bagel, coffee or newspaper. I try to carry only small amounts of cash. Paying by credit card is handy. However, there goes my name and identification numbers to the cashier and computer system. I believe that most people are not thieves or muggers. Still, I try to always shop in well-lit areas in neighborhoods where I see policemen on occasion. I feel most secure and safest when I have a male friend who loves to drive, shop, take my car to the garage and pick up my cleaning, paying for all services and purchases along the way.

So, Can You, Should You, Might You or Will You?!?!

Checklist of Choices

☐ When withdrawing money from your bank, hold on tightly to your cash. Rush quickly to your car. If walking, hurry home as fast as you can.

☐ If you are a lady, wear your purse around your neck and chest and hold it tightly. Only a wrestler or man with scissors would be able to get your purse and wallet.

- [ ] Dress shabbily when you shop. Don't wear diamonds, gold jewelry or a fur coat. A beige trench coat is a good choice.

- [ ] Pay by cheque if this an option and leave all of your money and credit cards at home. Be aware that you must expose your name and address.

- [ ] Be like a wolf and travel in a pack. Meet others at the cash register before pulling out your wallet and showing your money.

- [ ] Look forward to when you qualify for "Meals on Wheels" for delivery of your food. You will be paying an agency only once a month. But, will they bring French toast and cocoa at 2 a.m.?

- Live in the country and create your own supplies. Grow vegetables, milk cows and keep chickens. You will reduce the size of your shopping list and need to handle money.

- Cultivate dinner dates. Choose companions who love to take care of the bill and also leave the tip.

4. STANDING IN LINE-UPS

I expect line-ups in my life. They exist when I shop for groceries, go to the bank or get gas for my car. Even buying a ticket for a movie, purchasing a cup of coffee or arranging my funeral requires some waiting for service. I am usually not accompanied by another person. So, I must endure standing or sitting alone and amuse myself.

I recently had to fast for twelve hours before an ultrasound test at a hospital. I had to wait 40 minutes for the technician to do this procedure. Then, I was to proceed to another room for a blood test.

I was told that the waiting period was a minimum of one and a half hours. By this time, I was starving and I chose to go for breakfast and keep my blood to myself.

Another headache is dealing with line-ups at airports. I try to travel lightly but I still have to carry at least one suitcase and one overnight bag plus my purse. Announcements can break the monotony. But, porters do not move one's luggage forward as one moves through each line-up.

When I shop for groceries, I worry about my melting ice-cream and frozen vegetables as I wait in line. Those families with 75 items in their cart can take quite awhile to pass through the cashier.

Even when telephoning the government or an insurance company for information, we are put on hold after enduring the long list of recorded selections. At least, in the comfort of my home, I can sit down and have a cup of tea as I rest the telephone on my shoulder and wait for an operator. I manage these waiting times by viewing them as opportunities to develop patience. I can read, meditate or do a crossword puzzle until a person is available to provide service. In addition, I can learn skills in standing plus walking slowly when in a line-up outside my home.

So, Can You, Should You, Might You or Will You?!?!

Checklist of Choices

☐ Wait and wait and wait. As time goes by, know that eventually you will be first in line, unless the store closes first.

☐ Use the time to meditate or pray. Hope for a bit of speed in the flow of your line-up.

☐ Always carry a cell phone and laptop computer. You can then play games and e-mail your friends.

- [ ] In addition, carry some reading material. Read your article on self-love, your "To-Do" list or a book of short stories.

- [ ] Remember your last holiday at the seashore. Feel the ocean breeze. Taste the salt of the sea. Plan to visit a travel agent at times when there is no line-up.

- [ ] Smile and talk to strangers behind and ahead of you in the line-up. You might have time to begin a meaningful relationship.

- [ ] Count clouds or stars if you are outdoors or near a window. You can also compare the numbers of people behind and ahead of you in line.

- Choose stores with interesting items near the cash register. Supermarkets often have chocolate bars and magazines like *Oprah* or *Time* to nourish your body and soul and keep you informed of current events.

- Shop only around midnight. There will be no line-ups. However, most places will be closed.

5. GETTING TO THOSE APPOINTMENTS

I can easily slip into extreme panic and self-pity when I have a throbbing toothache, a swollen right ankle or chest pains in the night. I am so grateful when I call the emergency phone number of my dentist or doctor and the nurse says, "come right over, we have staff here to take care of you." My heart sings. A routine medical check-up can also feel urgent if I have waited six months for an appointment, have a long list of ailments and need many prescriptions filled.

Then, the fun begins as I face the challenge of getting there if I am in extreme pain and need some help. I have often called a neighbor or friend for a lift to an appointment and got only an answering machine or busy signal. Phoning for a taxi puts me on the waiting list for the next available car.

Despite sharp pain in my back, ankle or fingernail, I know I must find the strength to comb my hair, put on some clothes and grab my purse. I distract myself from the pain so that I can plan my journey to the doctor or dentist by getting my endorphins flowing. I enjoy the purring of my cats as they brush against me, a small but valued pleasure as I struggle with my discomfort. I recall singing a rousing chorus of "he-he and ho-ho" led by a clown with a red rubber nose at my local Laughter Club. I can also smile a tiny bit when I remember Woody Allen's attempt to impress his blind date in *"Play It Again Sam"* as he reached for a record and it flew out of the jacket and traveled across the room.

I then breathe deeply, focus on the healing hands of my dentist or doctor and stroll or crawl to my car if I am able to manage this on my own. Since my medical assistants do not have offices near a bus stop, I must drive, get a lift from someone or take a taxi to their offices.

After arriving, there is the challenge of finding a parking spot and then getting to the waiting room. A line-up of patients is inevitable. I take a handful of Tylenol to survive the time until the smiling dentist or doctor appears. I keep a book of cartoons in my purse and try to read a few and chuckle a bit. I pray that he or she will get rid of my pain immediately and that I can get home safely on my own or with the help of a friend.

So, Can You, Should You, Might You or Will You?!?!

Checklist of Choices

☐ Go immediately to your bed. Weep for awhile, then call the doctor or dentist for an appointment.

☐ Forget your pain. Imagine the Caribbean as you sit on a soft deck chair with ten beach boys waiting on you.

☐ Stay home and suffer if you can barely move. Take a sleeping pill and wait for morning. Have pleasant dreams. Hope that your pain flies away in the night.

- [ ] Comfort yourself before dressing and travelling. Apply a heating pad or ice cubes to your pain. Take drugs of your choice and hug your pillow. Recall some funny jokes.

- [ ] Call 911 for an ambulance if you must. Don't forget your wallet and your health insurance card.

- [ ] Call and treat yourself to a taxi. Even if it costs $100, you deserve it. Take a book of cartoons or your teddy bear with you.

- [ ] Get to the lobby of your building or front porch of your house and tell your story to each person that you encounter. Hope that someone will offer you a lift.

- [ ] When no one offers you a lift and you are short of cash, hitchhike. Be ready to use your pepper spray if the person who picks you up is wearing sunglasses at night and flirts with you.

☐ Pray for the return of house calls by doctors. Remain optimistic despite cuts in health care.

☐ Be strong and healthy. Eat well, exercise, count your blessings and value your friends and family. See your doctor and dentist only when you experience extreme pain.

6. STRUGGLING WITH SUPERINTENDENTS

I can change a light bulb, remove a spot from my carpet and put a new filter in my humidifier. However, I still frequently need my superintendent. There are times when my tap won't stop running, my cat is stuck in the chandelier or the refrigerator is so hot that everything in my freezer is melting. In addition, I cannot replace my screens in the windows after I remove them for washing and my nerves get jangled when I look at the fuse box. I know that the superintendent is my employee. Yet, I often feel that I am bothering him and his wife when I ask for help. I know that my leaky faucet is not as important as elevators that won't move or a fire alarm system that goes off in the night. However, I feel that I require and deserve his assistance after he has coped with building emergencies.

I ponder why superintendents are more attentive when I call on them with a male companion at my side. Since I am usually facing the superintendent on my own, I try to find a building with a husband-and-wife team who are kind, understanding and friendly. I once forgot my keys and had to call them at midnight. I learned that ringing their buzzer after dark was not appreciated. Our relationship was never the same after that.

My most terrible experience was living in a building where the superintendent hated cats. Whenever I needed to call him for a repair, it was necessary to hide my beloved pet and all his belongings in the bedroom. I also had to vacuum and dust in order to remove fur balls and cat hair. Lighting incense and spraying the rooms with a pleasant vanilla scent were part of my routine. I prayed that the cat would not meow. When I moved, he charged me a fee of $100 to fumigate my apartment, claiming cat-related cleanup fees. I did not recommend that building to my friends or enemies. Since I cannot always afford a repairman or call a handy friend, I do my best to be friendly to my superintendent. I never forget to give him chocolates, wine or nuts and a card at Christmas.

So, Can You, Should You, Might You or Will You?!?!

Checklist of Choices

☐ Check out both the health and personality of your superintendent. Spend as much time getting to know him as you do looking at the layout of your apartment.

☐ If the superintendent coughs and sneezes when you appear with five cat hairs on your shoulder, look for another building.

☐ Keep articles and lists of Internet sites that give you practical tips on repairs that you can do on your own. Did you know that baking soda and vinegar clear a drain?

- Keep a ladder, flashlight, candles, fuses and plunger in your cupboard. A book of cartoons and a package of cookies can also be helpful.

- Be prepared to pay repairmen to come in at times when your superintendent is off duty. Getting a plumber on Sunday night or Christmas is difficult and double or triple the usual fee.

- If you superintendent is an ogre, get your mail only at midnight. You will avoid encountering him in the lobby.

- Take a friend when you ask your superintendent for help. Expect better service if he is over six feet tall and muscular.

- Move to a bungalow or house. You will not have a superintendent. You can do all of the repairs by yourself or pay for services.

7. COPING WITH WINTER

I live in southern Ontario in Canada. Snow, sleet and cold air will cover my world many times between November and March. I find myself at home alone a lot. Winter in some areas of Canada and the United States may present you with only heavy rainfall and damp air; this too can chill your bones and keep you indoors.

When I was a child, I remember my mother bundling me up in two sweaters, woolen slacks and a powder-blue outfit of thick leggings, a long coat and a heavy hat with ear flaps. Boots, a scarf and mittens completed the ensemble. I was warm even though I could barely walk with so much clothing. Play was impossible.

As an adult, I find that the necessity of many layers of clothing still persists. I omit the leggings but always wear a vest and a sweater for chilly rooms at home or in the workplace. Every outing requires a coat, boots, a hat, gloves and a scarf. When entering a store, I need to peel off a few items to avoid excessive perspiration. When I return to the outdoors, I must bundle up again. An extra seat at the movies is a blessing. I can store my hat, coat and scarf beside me rather than on my lap. This leaves room for my bag of popcorn and bottle of water.

Winter's second major challenge is driving on slippery roads and facing traffic delays due to accidents. I have spent many hours sitting in my car, roasting in my boots, sweaters and coat. Waiting in the cold for a bus in the cold is also an ordeal. However, I need to apply much less blusher as my cheeks become naturally rosy from the cold wind.

Winter, however, is also a season of exquisite visual beauty. I am able to enjoy white, pale blue and gray blanketing my environment and experience great sensual delight. Sparkling icicles and trees coated with fluffy snow are lovely sights to behold. When the snow is clean right after it falls, I hate to take steps onto the pure surface and leave dark footprints. Nevertheless, I prefer to stay indoors as much as possible. I don't ski or skate. Walking without slipping and sliding is my major athletic achievement. I survive the winter by viewing it as a time of opportunity to have extra time inside my home for writing and painting. I wear a warm velour robe and slippers with socks to feel snug and cozy.

So, Can You, Should You, Might You or Will You?!?!

Checklist of Choices

☐ Avoid making a medical or dental appointment between November and March unless you are in unbearable pain. Take a Tylenol and get under the covers.

- Decorate all rooms in your home with cactus plants and pictures of beaches. Draw the drapes and pretend you live in Florida when there are no hurricanes.

- Stock up on quilts, electric blankets and fuel for your furnace. Don't forget hot chocolate and chicken soup.

- Be sure you like your winter coat, boots, hat, scarf and gloves. You will wear them a lot. Choose bright colors like hot pink and lime green.

- Wear your blouse or shirt from Hawaii every other day. Know that summer will come again.

☐ Love your car if you have one. Get a tune-up and antifreeze. Check the heater, defroster and windshield wipers regularly. Remember to get gas.

☐ Give yourself extra time to get anywhere. Carry CDs and cassettes plus a snack of apples and peanuts. A chocolate bar or fudge can sweeten your journey.

☐ Enjoy the beauty of falling snowflakes. The best view is from lying on your couch cuddled under an afghan.

☐ Relentlessly pursue a partner for those freezing nights. Hope springs eternal. Or cuddle up with a heating pad and a teddy bear.

PART 4

ON RELATING TO OTHER PEOPLE

After learning to love my own company and mastering techniques for doing the chores, I turned my attention towards my personal relationships. I treasure my solitude. I know that I am never entirely alone at home since I have the company of two friendly felines. However, I still need and want to be with other people some of the time in order to hear the spoken word rather than meows and purrs. By being open to social interaction in a variety of forms, I am able to live with occasional loneliness, banish a sense of isolation and prevent high anxiety.

Friendships are essential for maintaining my sanity during rough times and enriching my experiences during good times. Support and sharing are anchors that keep me from drifting out to sea when storms are brewing. I have one friend I can call at any hour; this is so helpful during a bout of insomnia around midnight. Celebrating birthdays with a meal at a Thai restaurant is a ritual I cherish with a special person. I value my brother and sister-in-law for their caring, commitment to my welfare, and material assistance. An annual family barbecue is a special event with much food and affection.

Cultivating relations with acquaintances is something I do to expand my social network. I feel a deep bond with a handyman neighbor who gives me a sense of security when I need him to change a fluorescent tube in my washroom light fixture or help me with hanging drapes; these tasks are not part of the superintendent's services. Smiling and exchanging a greeting with a stranger can bring warmth and brightness to a dull day. It may be my companion on an elevator or someone walking their dog. I exercise caution if he or she is wearing sunglasses at night or clutching the leash of a growling pit bull.

Unless I attend an event with a friend, I must cultivate my courage to face social situations by myself. With no constant companion to support me before, during and after many social occasions, I face the challenges of new values, rules of etiquette and lifestyle trends. I thought I had a lovely new friend until she constantly criticized me for polluting the environment when I discarded the plastic containers from my tomatoes and strawberries. When I date a car salesman, I must refer to the older automobiles as pre-owned instead of as used cars. I envy my divorced and widowed friends for their specialized support groups. Where are the groups for single people who have lost a lover? Our society frowns upon wrinkles and worships youth. I refuse to buy the face creams of companies that promote anti-aging with models who appear to be under 21 years of age. I have earned every wrinkle and do not worship youth. All I want is a bit of moisture plus sun protection for my skin, not a face of a teen-ager.

I strive to focus on cheerful social situations. I am constantly grateful for the numerous social opportunities for those of us who live alone by choice or circumstance, unavailable to our parents' generation or pioneers who lived one hundred years ago. A few options that can help us with our social life are such activities as: using the telephone, connecting by computer, learning from television and radio, sending real letters that can arrive in only a few days, taking courses, and joining clubs. Walking on sidewalks, driving on paved roads or taking public transportation sure beats weeks of traveling in a covered wagon for days to make contact with another person.

1. DINING WITH OTHERS

I like to eat with friends. Sharing a meal is a nourishing way to interact with others, receiving food for my body plus social stimulation. Shopping and cooking chores are eliminated if we eat out at a restaurant.

Nevertheless, when in the company of others, I expect comments on my selections. People tend to have strong views on how to eat properly. I have often gotten indigestion after a dinner with a companion who lectured me on the evils of red meat, white bread and salt as I munched on a delicious pepperoni pizza with anchovies.

Magazines and newspapers constantly present articles on the best diet for health, happiness and abs of steel. I am always challenged to find the truth as I wade through the latest research. There are viewpoints both for and against most foods. Shall I coat my bread with butter or margarine? Will I drink diet pop with aspartame or regular pop with sugar? Should I eat Atlantic or Pacific salmon? In addition, many people are obsessed with watching the calories and carbohydrates in their food and are also concerned about their cholesterol.

When I throw a dinner party in my home, I can select the menu and the guests. I want friends and family who will be tolerant, accepting and appreciative of everything on my dinner table plus the tastes of the other people. Guests under ten years of age usually fit this bill. I also try to avoid conflict and extra work by inviting my vegetarian and meat-eating friends on different nights. However, if I have only one vegetarian guest, I serve a bean and grain casserole as well as steaks or roast beef for the carnivores.

Yet, I feel entitled to be lax about what I eat on occasion, especially outside of my home. Since I do not have a partner who is eating the same foods as myself, thus giving me support in my choices, I strive to be healthy plus satisfy my senses. After all, I am the only one who is living with my stomach and digestive system.

So, Can You, Should You, Might You or Will You?!?!

Checklist of Choices

☐ Dare to order a glass of tap water to quench your thirst. It is cheaper than Perrier or Evian water.

☐ Choose a glass of sparkling white wine although the others select red for the health of their hearts. Be prepared for a comment on the sugar count of your wine.

☐ Enjoy your white garlic bread smothered in butter. Also, select either a piece of stone ground whole wheat bread or a seven-grain roll for your fibre needs.

☐ Order a filet mignon steak wrapped in bacon. Ignore the glares from your pals as they eat their vegetarian pizza, steamed fish, green salads and brown rice with beans.

☐ Request coffee and cream after the meal even if your companions choose green tea with lemon on the side. Ignore comments about the negative effects of caffeine on your nervous system and fertility.

☐ Order a piece of chocolate cake and strawberry ice cream with extra whipped cream for dessert. You deserve a sweet dessert after a lecture on the evils of sugar.

2. SPEAKING POLITICALLY CORRECTLY

 Since I live alone, I need and value the company of my family, friends and acquaintances on a regular basis. I have worked hard to acquire skills in communicating effectively, to say what I mean, to express my needs, and to share anger appropriately. Reading self-help books and belonging to groups like Toastmasters have helped me to speak sincerely and eloquently.

We live in a society where we are constantly reminded to speak and write correctly with sensitivity to individual differences. I ponder my choice of words when I am communicating with such individuals as: the physically challenged, feminists, gays and lesbians, immigrants, youth, and seniors. Animal activists require that we speak with gentle tones and act with compassion towards animals. Incorrect use of the spoken and written word can result in getting sued, fired, charged, jailed or at least cause people to snicker or make sarcastic remarks.

I dare not call a person "crippled" when speaking to someone with a limp or use slang words such as "wop" when addressing an Italian. When I am in a situation with militant feminists or others who demand non-sexist language, I use words like "humankind" rather than "mankind" and "chairperson" instead of "chairman." Of course, I address the females with the title of "Ms." I am particularly offended when a salesperson asks for my marital status if I am purchasing a scarf and using my credit card. When he or she asks me if I am a "Miss" or

"Mrs." as they fill out the sales slip, I hold back a silent scream.

Many people are obsessed with avoiding offending others. It is tough to talk spontaneously. I cannot always get my message across non-verbally by dancing, playing the guitar, using sign language or e-mailing a picture on my computer. Such non-verbal means of communication are especially awkward or inappropriate when relating to my boss or doctor. So, I read current books on etiquette and do my best to speak politically correctly.

So, Can You, Should You, Might You or Will You?!?!

Checklist of Choices

☐ Enjoy speaking to your pets, plants and computer. They will accept any words you choose to use.

- [ ] Remain silent and wait for someone else to speak first when you are with others. Then you can listen to their choice of words.

- [ ] Hold your tongue when a verbally abusive person talks to you. Reply in Swahili to discourage any further conversation. Or, turn off your hearing aid if you wear one.

- [ ] Carry and consult a multi-lingual dictionary when in doubt as to which words to use. A book of etiquette can also be helpful.

- [ ] Always note if a lady prefers to be addressed as Ms., Mrs., Dr., or Madam. Also, don't stand too close or fondle her in order to avoid a charge of sexual harassment.

- [ ] Be careful when you talk about your designer clothes. They might be made in a country where children were paid two cents an hour. Tuck in those labels or wear a brooch or handkerchief over the designer's name.

- [ ] Talk on the telephone instead of writing—assuming you can get through to a real person. If you speak incorrectly, at least your words won't exist in print to be used against you in court.

3. LAUGHING AGAIN AFTER YOUR DIVORCE

I have never married and so have not experienced the pain of divorce. However, I have had dates and relationships with divorced men and friendships with women who went through divorces.

    I have also known the agony after the end of long-term relationships. I was involved with a legally separated man who said that he expected his divorce papers within two months. The legal process took two years. Much of the sparkle of our romance went down the drain as his good moods and finances slowly slipped away.

I know that the loss of a partner can flood our lives with feelings of sadness, depression, anger, rage and even some guilt. If the choice to divorce was not mutual and you preferred to keep the relationship, the distress can be as sharp as an attack of appendicitis. If your children are no longer with you, except for occasional visits, you can feel great loneliness within your solitary home. Although a new and happier life eventually will come to you, there is no escape from a period of angst. The "gay divorcee" probably exists only in the movies or at least quite awhile after the legal and financial threads are tied together to support your survival.

Don't miss appointments with your lawyer, accountant, barber or hairdresser. Hope can and must be found in the ruins of a life without a mate even if a large shovel or bulldozer is required to clear the way towards your new beginnings. Be open to every smile, snicker and chuckle to receive warmth and comfort. You will know you have arrived when you can laugh again while you remember all of the things that you disliked about your ex-spouse as you throw your wedding ring out the window. Or, sell the ring for some extra money and treat yourself to a facial, massage and a large container of chocolate ice cream.

So, Can You, Should You, Might You or Will You?!?!

Checklist of Choices

☐ Allow yourself to cry and experience the blues. Since you are alone, you can howl at the moon and sob all night.

☐ Feel your anger. Punch pillows rather than your pet or plants. Write hate letters to express your negative emotions but don't mail them to your ex-spouse.

☐ Enjoy your freedom to sleep all over the bed. You can also keep the window open, retire when you wish and sleep until noon. Leave extra food for your pets.

- [ ] Wear your old asexual flannel pajamas to bed. Hug your teddy bear or the other pillow. Invite your pets to fill his or her space.

- [ ] Be grateful that you don't have to shave your legs constantly (ladies) or your beard (gentlemen) in order to impress your mate.

- [ ] Join a support group for people who are divorced. You will then have a social outing at least once a week.

- [ ] Plan the next 30 outings with your children to such places as McDonald's, the video arcade, the movies or the family psychotherapist. Your week-ends will be full.

- [ ] Look forward to your next meaningful relationship, even if it is with your therapist, lawyer or accountant or for awhile.

4. FACING THE FUTURE AS A WIDOW OR WIDOWER

 I once had a long-term relationship with a man who died suddenly from a heart attack a few years after we broke up. We had remained close friends. After the initial shock, I had to wade through a variety of feelings such as denial, anger and sadness before acceptance flowed through me.

When you divorce, your ex-spouse is likely to still be around in your life even though you might wish he or she were in northern Alaska. This is definitely a fact when you share custody of children. However, as you face the permanent loss of a loved one, there are mountains of emotional, legal, and financial concerns that can overwhelm you. I feel deep compassion for those of you who are facing the future after the loss of your spouse, especially if you had many years as a happy couple.

You might ask why bad things happen to a good person—namely you and your deceased partner. This is definitely a question with no clear answer. Rather, you might focus upon what you can do to deal with your loss. You can eventually find the power to shape your reactions to face your loss and shape your life in new and satisfying ways. You deserve as much self-love, self-help and social support as you can find. Cater to all levels of your being—physical, emotional, social, intellectual, and spiritual. Be a snail. Move along in your grieving process at your own rate. Believe that you deserve to see the sun again and find new hobbies, interests and friends.

You will recover from your loss and join the ranks of those of us who successfully live alone.

So, Can You, Should You, Might You or Will You?!?!

Checklist of Choices

☐ Keep a lot of boxes of Kleenex in your home. Let the tears flow. Change your sweater when it becomes cold and damp from your teardrops.

☐ Take comfort from your sympathy cards. Pay attention to kind messages and pictures of flowers, bridges, and clouds. Know that people care about you and your loss.

- [ ] Keep a journal. Let yourself experience and express all of your sadness. It is okay to grieve for only one month if you are a quick mourner or seven years if you are slow in shedding sadness.

- [ ] Enjoy little pleasures. Let your grandchildren, the dog and cat sleep in your bed. Wear the red tie with rockets (that she hated) or the soft housecoat with holes (that he hated).

- [ ] Treat your body to anything it craves in any amount. Try chocolates, ice cream, and soft quilts. Warm baths, soft music, and teddy bears can also help.

- [ ] Sort his or her clothes and things only when you are ready. Goodwill and the Red Cross are not going out of business and will accept your donations any time.

- [ ] Join a support group for widows and widowers. Weeping together can lighten your load. Smiling and laughter can also occur at any time.

- [ ] Carry a book of cartoons with you, even to the shower, as you are ready to smile again. Laughter will come later.

- [ ] Visit with your lawyer and financial advisor. See yourself as smart, capable, and able to handle your affairs even if your spouse kept all of your papers a secret from you.

- [ ] Go for drives and dinners with your children and friends. Anyone who offers an outing is acceptable when your knees are wobbly.

- [ ] Turn towards spiritual assistance. There is always refuge in the Lord, any goddess, angels, or your Higher Self. Even Voodoo is okay. Read the Bible or a book of recipes for chocolate chip cookies, carrot cake, or blueberry muffins.

5. CAN YOU SPARE SOME TIME? VOLUNTEER!

Helping others is guaranteed to help you forget your problems. Whether you are coping with the loss of a loved one, facing unemployment, having problems with your boss or struggling with a sick pet, your troubles will run away as you focus upon other people and their needs. If you are facing a blind man and assisting him with shopping or taking a woman in a wheelchair to the bank, your own load of chores will feel much lighter as you count your blessings. As you listen to a bruised woman who has been beaten by her husband, your backache will hurt less. If you lead an illiterate person into the world of reading and writing, your heart will sing. A regular commitment to some form of volunteer work can give you social contact, perspective on your burdens, a reduction in feelings of loneliness and a sense of fulfillment and usefulness in your life.

I have recently retired. When I worked full-time, I asked myself how I could possibly find time to help others. Evenings were reserved for recovery from my job and preparation for the next day. After all, I did need to relax my weary bones and muscles, prepare and eat some dinner, be a couch potato for awhile, find a few clean clothes and prepare a lunch. Weekends required attention to chores like laundry, shopping for groceries and pet food plus attending to a touch of housework.

On occasion, I was able to find some small ways of helping others with little acts of kindness. I would smile at a weary cashier at the store or send a cheque to an animal shelter. I would help a stranger who slipped on the ice, laugh at my boss's corny jokes or telephone a sick friend. For awhile, I used my breaks at the library where I worked to help a child learn how to read. I thus contributed to an increase in the circulation statistics when she began checking out books. When I was younger, I used one day off to create a list of suppliers of crafts materials for an organization. This gave me knowledge and skills that led to a new job. Giving even a little bit of time, money or energy to others can make all the difference to a needy person or animal.

So, Can You, Should You, Might You or Will You?!?!

Checklist of Choices

☐ Be a foster parent to a puppy or a kitten. This is only a short-term commitment. All you can lose is your heart.

- [ ] Knit scarves for the homeless. You might only have the energy to do two rows a night after working on the computer all day. You can make a long scarf in 352 days.

- [ ] Send a cheque to a charity. Use your leftover savings instead of depositing them in your bank. Even five dollars is okay. A little more is desirable if you wish to help earthquake victims.

- [ ] Make a regular commitment to do volunteer work at a hospital, shelter or agency, when you are able to find the time. This will get you out of the house and expand your social network.

- [ ] Leave a box of candies in the box for the food bank. This will help your waistline and sweeten the life of a needy person.

- [ ] Donate old books to your local library. I hope your back will be strong enough to carry them. If not, deliver one or two items at a time.

- ☐ Clear the clutter from your closets and give away old clothes. Your pet will have more room to play and nap. This option may be pursued around midnight when you are at loose ends.

- ☐ Send out prayers for peace on earth. You can do this any time of day or night. It is action that is free of charge.

6. GROWING OLDER WITH STYLE

Eventually, we all will lose our youth. I sometimes find myself in a state of high anxiety when I imagine my golden years without a spouse to help me to survive and thrive. Who will open the tin of cat food when my fingers are knotted with arthritis? Who will make me chicken soup when I am trapped in bed due to a strained back? Who will take me to the park when I have to push my walker and carry a cane? What will I do when I can no longer read regular print–even with my trifocals?

I remind myself that we always have a choice as to how we react to any challenging situation. After all, I know that I can buy the tins of cat food with the flip-top lids that require no can opener. I can call a Chinese restaurant for delivery of great chicken noodle or won ton soup. I can tell my date that we must switch from dancing to concerts where there will be comfortable seats to rest our aching muscles. My local library has a great selection of large-print books and will also deliver to the housebound. Magnifying glasses are available in stores.

I once sprained my back and could not bend over to feed my cat. He ate from dishes placed on the kitchen floor. I had to call my neighbor to put his bowls for food and water on the counter. This room was open to the living-dining area. The cat coped. He jumped from the floor to a chair, hopped onto a table and then leaped to the counter. I then knew that he could eat and drink and I was also free from worrying about stepping on his tail while he met his needs.

Occasionally, I feel jealous when I see old couples holding hands and wobbling together down the street into the sunset or to the doctor's office. At such times I switch my attention to the fact that fine wines and perfumes improve with age. I hope that I will be able to feel and look my best, accepting the effects of time rolling by as it leaves marks on my body. I buy large tubes of creams for sore muscles and wrinkles. I am constantly building up a rich bank of relationships, hobbies, healthy habits and money to maintain my independence. I renew my vows to count my blessings on a daily basis and maintain a positive and jolly attitude.

So, Can You, Should You, Might You or Will You?!?!

Checklist of Choices

☐ Rush out and take that seminar on the ageless and timeless body so you will be strong and beautiful forever. Also attend a lecture on money management. Let hope spring eternally.

☐ Subscribe immediately to that magazine with the feature story on reversing the aging process. Watch videos on blooming baby boomers like Jane Fonda.

☐ Visit the health food store frequently and buy all of the vitamins, green tea and bran that you can afford.

- [ ] Learn to love broiled chicken without the fat, steamed fish and beans instead of roast beef, french fries and croissants. Join a gym and lift weights. Walk around the block at least once a week.

- [ ] Feel no shame, gentlemen, if Viagra is your pill of preference. Carry a fan, ladies, for the times when those hot flashes strike. A thin paperback book can also do the trick.

- [ ] Bond with friendly doctors, dentists, chiropractors and optometrists. A massage therapist who does house calls can be a soothing blessing if you can afford one.

- [ ] Perk up your appearance. Try a blond toupée. Streak your hair orange. Whiten your teeth. Be grateful that you still have teeth and hair. Or, remove all mirrors from your home.

- [ ] Pray for the delivery of the government promises of increases in health and pension benefits. Reduced taxes would also be nice.

- [ ] Cultivate relationships with a financial planner and bank manager. As the Duchess of Windsor said, "you can never be too rich or too thin."

- [ ] Spend winters in Florida, if you are from a place where it snows. This will cut down on your spending for boots, coats, scarves, sweaters and gloves. You will only need a light coat for cool tropical evenings.

7. FINDING FRIENDSHIPS

 I have a magnet on my refrigerator that defines a friend as "someone who knows you as you are, understands where you've been, accepts whom you've become, and still, gently invites you to grow." I seek and cultivate friends who are like this. They are the diamonds, emeralds and rubies, the precious people who add sparkle and warmth to my life. My friends encourage me through rough moments and add stimulation and entertainment to enrich my life.

My two cats are great company. They are my little prisoners of love, always at home ready to play and shower me with affection. However, I still need people and get by with help from my friends.

I treasure Barbara who will always listen to me when I feel blue; she is sympathetic when I am having a bad cat day after one of my felines throws up on the fresh laundry. Barb and I also share a love of walking in the woods. Helena and I are bonded together with our passion for cats and creating art. Jo-an is a special lady who encourages and supports my writing. Maria is a friend in her late eighties who continues to paint and is an inspiring model of creativity and strength. Lina is a wonderful lady who supports me in everything I feel and do; her children, Matthew and Isabella, create cheerful greeting cards for me throughout the year. Shirley and I share a love of jazz. Eliza and I love concerts, cats and writing.

Marianne and Joh are passionate photographers who present beautiful slide shows on their travels in Europe and art photography with every dinner party. Francois and Wanda cook divine meals such as roast chicken and bake fabulous desserts like a blueberry pie that bursts with flavor. My brother, Sheldon, is also my friend. He does my taxes and always has extra dollars to help me with unexpected expenses such as my heating unit crashing in the winter.

It is challenging to keep old friends and find new ones. People move away to new homes, jobs, and spouses. They can run away when their interest in you dissolves. If you are from a functional family that is loving, nurturing and supportive and accepts your true, real, and loveable self, your needs for friends will be zero, minimal or sporadic. The rest of us need to hunt for supportive friendships and nourish them with devotion. We must look for people and then choose wisely, treasuring those friends who stick and stay for awhile.

So, Can You, Should You, Might You or Will You?!?!

Checklist of Choices

☐ Express your appreciation of your friends. Send them a singing telegram, bones for their dogs or greeting cards with poems created by you.

- [ ] Select people who are as fit and healthy as Jane Fonda so they will last as friends until you are old and gray. Toddlers are good bets.

- [ ] Attend authors' book launches to meet literary types. Attend openings at art galleries to mix with artists. Enjoy free wine and cheese.

- [ ] Feed your friends to nourish your bonds. Do it potluck style to save your time, energy and money.

- [ ] Take courses to meet others with similar interests. Try mountain climbing, gift-wrapping or playing the violin. You have no partner who will criticize you.

- [ ] Have at least 16 pen pals to contact by e-mail or snail mail. Then, you can contact others any time. For hugs, pick people who will meet you in real life.

☐ Join groups. Consider art galleries, Weight Watchers, stamp clubs, or UFO Societies. Being part of a group is comforting.

☐ Be your own best friend. Smile at yourself in the mirror. Wrap you arms around yourself for a loving embrace. Indulge in treats like Belgian chocolates and a cashmere scarf.

☐ Seek people who feed your soul, are sensitive to your feelings, and entertain you with a hearty laugh Find friends who are like Leonard Cohen, Oprah, and the cast of the *"Royal Canadian Air Farce."*

PART 5

ON FINDING COMFORT FROM MACHINES

We don't realize how much we rely on machines and electricity until we don't have them. My home is full of mechanical helpmates, devices that make life easier, more comfortable and entertaining. I love my kettle, toaster oven, television, radio, computer and even my vacuum cleaner.

Several years ago, there was a power blackout in Ontario and the northeastern United States. I remember the library, where I worked, closed early since most jobs depended upon the use of computers to process items, find materials and check out books and other media. Even the most experienced librarian cannot remember all of the titles, authors and subjects listed in the catalogue.

When I got home and entered my apartment, it was silent without the radio that I usually left on to comfort my cats whenever I went out. I could not make my usual cup of tea and slice of toast or check my telephone answering machine messages and e-mails on the computer. I opened my refrigerator and almost wept as I knew my milk, cottage cheese and yogurt would soon become sour. Several containers of salads and fish did not look too healthy either. In the freezer, trays of ice cubes were transforming to puddles of water and my packages of fish, chicken, frozen vegetables and a tub of ice cream were well on their way to oblivion.

I was greatly relieved to find that the telephone worked and human contact was possible. I called my friend, Peter, who is in his seventies. He lives on the fourteenth floor of a high-rise. He still had taken his dog Charley out for a walk, despite the heat. After all, the canine had to do his daily poop. I telephoned several other friends and we shared our concerns about food and what we would do in long night ahead, if the blackout continued.

As twilight descended, I scurried about searching for candles, matches and a flashlight. I had no batteries. So, I was glad that a neighbor had an extra flashlight to give me. I did not look forward to walking up and down four flights of stairs, since there was no elevator service, then driving in pitch black to find an open store.

Dinner was a tuna sandwich with warm and wilted lettuce and apple juice. I missed television, my usual companion for an evening at home alone. However, I began to enjoy my cozy bedroom, lit by the soft glow of many candles. My cats curled into comforting purring balls at my feet. I read by flashlight for a few hours. Every so often, I would take a break and shine the flashlight around the room. The cats delighted in leaping and chasing the light beams.

I realized that I could survive without my machines, at least for one evening and one night. However, I was full of joy when the power returned the next morning. I immediately turned on the air conditioner and popped a Chopin CD into my player. I then sat down with a freshly brewed cup of coffee and planned a dinner party where I could create sandwiches from my six loaves of thawed bread. With gratitude, I looked forward to sending and receiving e-mails again and watching television that evening. I was even eager to do some laundry and vacuuming.

1. WATCHING TV: LET ME COUNT THE WAYS

 My family was the first one on the street to get a television set in the 1950s when I was a child. I was very popular. My friends and neighbors would gather to watch the *Howdy Doody Show*. My brothers' friends rallied round to watch *Hopalong Cassidy* and *The Lone Ranger*. The *Ed Sullivan*, *Milton Berle* and *I Love Lucy* shows also drew large crowds.

I am now a visual person. I find television a wondrous window onto the world. I can always find shows that are informative, entertaining and even inspiring. When I am at home alone, this machine is a major pal. I am thrilled to catch the opening ceremonies of the Olympic Games and the Academy Awards.

I am not fussy about commercials. So, I use my VCR to tape movies and programs that I can watch at my convenience and skip the ads. I enjoy *Biography*, documentaries on nature and wildlife plus an occasional dose of comedy like *Frasier*.

In addition, I have found television helpful for survival. I used to have a job where I commuted from one city to another. I watched the weather network many times at night during the winter months. This was essential for guiding my daily travel plans, except when the weather forecast was wrong. I had no partner to give me rides to and from work when I could not face roads blanketed in snow and ice.

I miss the early days when there were only a few channels. I could quickly scan the *TV Guide*. Then, I would tape a few programs to entertain me the next day. Now, major concentration and decision-making are required. There can be at least 30 choices of programs listed for each half-hour. Many questions must be asked and answered. Am I picking a program covered by the cable company for my area? Are the codes for the channels the same as last week? Is the program I like still on? Did I set the timer correctly when I taped a program? Am I following the correct procedures for taping my chosen programs? Have I checked that the cats have not chewed the chaos of wires flowing from my television, DVD player and VCR? Did the felines pull out the plugs?

I know that I will face a major research project when I buy my next television. Besides examining picture and sound quality, ease of use and price, I will have to consider whether or not I want a flat-panel set, an LCD or plasma TV or a large screen of 60 inches or more. Will I need HD (high-definition) or ED (enhanced-definition), stretch and zoom modes or additional components like video inputs for better quality with equipment like DVD players, high-definition satellite receivers, and cable boxes? Then, I will have to ponder the possible choice of DCR (digital-cable-ready), a new type of HDTV ready for some digital programming with no additional devices.

For the moment, I am content with my simple television set, DVD player and VCR, except for the wires. I believe that television can be an enjoyable and useful machine for people who live alone. The trials and tribulations are worth it, as long as we make the correct choices and develop a few skills!

So, Can You, Should You, Might You or Will You?!?!

Checklist of Choices

☐ Read the blurbs on the programs in your television guide and color your choices in hot pink. Then you can find out whether your cable system gives you the channels for your choices. Or, list the channels you get.

- [ ] Purchase a magnifier to read what is on the buttons of your remote control. You alone have the power to press the buttons of your choice.

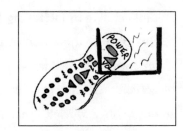

- [ ] Check the news on TV even If you read the newspaper. It is helpful to know if a war is declared, an election is called, or an ice storm is on its way. You can't always rely on your best friend to call you.

- [ ] Use the commercial breaks to get snacks. You can often have the time to feed your pets, take a quick shower or water the plants.

- [ ] Place cactus plants around the wires by your television set to prevent your pets from abusing them. Guests will also be stopped from tripping as they walk by.

- [ ] Ignore the descriptions of the wind patterns in Italy during the weather forecast—unless that is your vacation destination. However, you can use the images in your next painting if art is one of your hobbies.

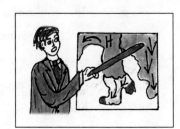

- [ ] Pay attention to details during the weather forecast. Make sure that you have watched the coverage for the city where you live rather than cottage country. Only you are at home to verify and adjust your travel plans to the forecast.

- [ ] Watch sports or soap operas all weekend. You have the freedom to please only yourself.

- [ ] Keep the blues at bay by watching comedy shows. Keep a few humorous videos or DVDs handy in case of a deep depression.

- [ ] Check the Internet for TV-related entertainment sites. See fan sites, episode guides, celebrity blogs and the *Internet Movie Database*.

- [ ] Rent videos and DVDs from your local store or borrow them from the public library. Thus, you avoid decision-making and challenges related to choosing and taping programs.

2. ENJOYING THE COMFORT OF A CAR

I learned to drive when I was 15 years old and immediately got my driver's license shortly after I turned 16. My first car was a black Mustang convertible with a white top. I was quite popular during the summer months. My friends and I would cruise the city streets with the top down and the radio blaring as we sipped our soft drinks. My choices turned towards more conservative models as the years went by, like a Chevrolet or Datsun.

I was never able to get jobs near my home when I joined the workforce and I faced variable schedules with evening and weekend shifts that never matched the times of the bus routes near my residence. So, a car was important to get me to and from work on time at my convenience.

I see my car as a welcome way for freedom. I can go places at any time. I am not chained to public transportation schedules. I can safely visit friends at midnight. I can do all of my chores at once, loading my parcels into the trunk. Taxis are expensive; the meter is still running when it is necessary to stop as my cat throws up on the seat on the way to the veterinarian's office. Gentlemen, a lady loves to be picked up for a date. A car makes a better impression than a bicycle, especially if she is wearing a dress and high heels.

Yes, there are substantial costs to owning a car. This is challenging since I am the only one paying my bills. I have to find the money to buy the car. There are many decisions I must make as I consider options and their cost: air-conditioning, satellite radio, a CD player, and leather or cloth seats. Gas, insurance and repairs for maintenance are rather necessary expenses. I strive for interior and exterior car washes every so often; this is desirable when I plan to have passengers. Thus, as a person on my own, I must carefully plan and examine my budget to pay for the freedom that my car gives me.

I sometimes consider alternatives to owning a car. I could travel by foot–strolling, running, jumping or doing somersaults as I move from place to place. These activities will count as endurance exercises to strengthen my heart. I must be careful since I do not have a partner at home to massage my feet. I have considered traveling by bicycle or motorcycle when I am feeling fit. I imagine the breeze caressing my hair. I would buy a black leather jacket, high boots and sunscreen to present a dashing image of a tan, healthy and glamorous lady.

I explore all types of public transportation such as buses, boats, planes and helicopters. I know that I would have to wear deodorant in the summer, hoping that others would do the same. I realize that it would sometimes be necessary to stand for awhile when there are no seats during rush hours.

If I use the subway, I could read en route. I would have to constantly switch my reading glasses and sunglasses as the trains go underground, above ground and below ground again. I cannot read without my spectacles, although I can look at pictures.

Even though I could use the extra money and contribute to fresher air by giving up my car, I prefer the comfort. It is divine to coast along in a warm or cool private bubble, sipping coffee and listening to a CD of Strauss waltzes. Instead of standing in shelters or on the street when it is raining or snowing, I can sit in traffic and catch up on the news or read a book.

So, Can You, Should You, Might You or Will You?!?!

Checklist of Choices

☐ Take a group of well-dressed men and women with you to the car dealer. Let them carry copies of *Consumer Reports* & *Lemon-Aid*. *Ms, GQ* & *Peanuts* might also help to get the salesperson in the right mood to give you a good price.

☐ Pick a color you like for your car. Black is a good choice if you attend many funerals. Metallic silver will glow in the dark.

- [ ] Choose a model that expresses the real you. Jeeps work well if you frequently visit jungles. A limousine with a chauffeur will enable you to do crosswords on your laptop on the way to work.

- [ ] Keep your car until it falls apart. Unless you are an extremely wealthy person, annual trade-ins are not necessary. Don't watch the commercials on TV as the new models are advertised.

- [ ] Feed your mechanic chocolate cookies. Throw in hand cream and soap and hope for a discount on car repairs.

- [ ] Watch the comings and goings of the sheiks in Iraq and Saudi Arabia. Your gas bill depends upon them. Learn Arabic to watch the oil prices at the source.

- [ ] Learn to operate the self-serve gas machine to save a few cents. Do wear gloves to catch the drips and don't forget to replace the cap for the gas tank.

☐ Select friends who own cars and
love to pick you up and drive
you anyplace at any hour of your
choosing. This will decrease your
gas bill.

3. DARING TO USE
THE TELEPHONE

I love and value my telephone. There is
nothing as comforting as a human voice and
dialogues compared to e-mail. I remember
long telephone conversations with my girl-
friends when I was a teenager. Even though
we were together at school all day, there was
still much to talk about, like boys, clothes,
homework and boys again. Since I had two
brothers, there was competition to use the telephone. My mother
had to set limits of 20 minutes to our calls when we were all home
at once and wanted to chat with our friends.

Now that I live on my own, I can speak for as long as I want.
I find the telephone essential for calling my family or friends when
I feel lonely. I love to share good news like a clean bill of health for
my cat after his annual check-up. I like to use the telephone to make
appointments, arrange dates and even get weather reports.

Similarly, I could not live without my answering machine. In addition to taking messages when I am out, it entertains my felines and lets me screen calls. Because so many calls are appeals for donations to charities, sales pitches from telemarketers or requests to do a survey, I usually wait before picking up the receiver. I want to make sure the caller is someone I know—like a friend, acquaintance or family member. Also, I don't mind if my dentist's receptionist is confirming an appointment.

I would rather hear a recorded message if I call someone who is away from the telephone rather than listening to endless ringing. When answering machines first appeared, I would often start speaking to other people's recorded message. I wondered why he or she would repeat the same message and fail to answer my questions. Now, I am telephone literate with these devices and bless them.

Besides annoyance at unsolicited telephone calls, my patience is exhausted when I am immediately put on hold and I am given some music to "entertain" me. When an automated receptionist gives so many instructions on which buttons to press for a directory of a company, government or movie theatre, I get quite overwhelmed. There are so many decisions to make before connecting to a real person.

If you must have access to a telephone at all times, choose a portable cell phone. These are also useful when you are making love or taking a shower. You can select cell phones with e-mail, a camera and Internet. A video phone would be suitable if you prefer to dress up when speaking on the telephone. Some cell phones are so compact that you can keep them in your make-up kit, jacket pocket or on your charm bracelet. It is helpful to have good eyesight and tiny fingers in order to press the correct buttons. Most of us would never think about living without a telephone. Yet, we often need a sense of humor to give our insides an internal jog as we laugh while waiting for service.

So, Can You, Should You, Might You or Will You?!?!

Checklist of Choices

☐ Speak quickly to record your message within 30 seconds when you get an answering machine. Do listen for the beep before you start talking.

☐ Have a playful attitude towards telephone tag. Giving and receiving recorded messages can go on for years.

☐ Listen carefully for instructions when calling a hospital or the government. Be sure to press the correct buttons or you will have to repeat your call .

- [ ] Enjoy the music when you are put on hold. Keep crayons and paper by the phone to express yourself while you wait. Red and black are good choices.

- [ ] Call from a phone booth when your partner has call display and you wish to keep your location a secret. This is also wise when speaking to a blind date.

- [ ] Comb your hair and wear a smart-looking sweater if you and the person you are calling have video phones. Winks and smiles can be added to your presentation. This is also important when calling your mother, if she is fussy about your appearance and social life.

- [ ] Choose friends, stores and doctors a few blocks from your home. Then you can just go out and talk to people unless they are busy on the telephone.

- [ ] You can always connect by writing a letter, sending a telegram or proceeding to e-mail.

4. CONFRONTING THE JOYS AND CHALLENGES OF A COMPUTER

I resisted buying a computer for many years. As a librarian, I was using a computer at work most of the day. I had a love-hate relationship with this machine. I knew that calls for service were frequent. Since I lived alone, I worried about being able to afford the cost of repairs and maintenance. I was anxious about whether I would have to call a technician to come to my home or take the computer to a shop. Would I be able to take my computer in for service and then be able to get the wires re-connected by myself? It was enough of an ordeal for me to take my toaster, vacuum cleaner or record player in for repairs. The instructions for refilling ink cartridges were also quite challenging to me. I planned to buy a kit to save money.

I finally relented. I bought a shelving unit, a computer system with a printer and a mouse pad and subscribed to an Internet service. My cats love looking at their reflections on the screen. Hairs continually appear on the keyboard, chair and mouse pad. So, I know that they continue to visit the computer when I am absent.

My time at home alone is now filled with a dazzling array of fascinating options when I choose to use my computer. It is so interesting to be able to read the news in papers from around the world. I love to look up book reviews, research movies and find recipes. Writing with a word processor is amazing. I can make corrections to a document or shift sentences and paragraphs in a flash. Using spell-check and playing with fonts are fun. Instant printing without running to a photocopier is a joy. It is lovely to send and receive e-mails for swift communication with friends all over the world. I save time and energy by making reservations for courses, travel and meals in restaurants. I can visit many other places in virtual reality like art galleries and museums that are beyond my travel budget in real life.

I recently added a scanner. I create and send greeting cards with pictures; this is rewarding and appreciated by my friends. I enjoy sending copies of photographs to friends, reproducing my paintings and scanning pages from books.

Owning a computer also presents challenges. While filling my cartridge, I once splattered black ink all over part of my kitchen. The permanent patterns on the wooden trims of my cupboards remind me of this nightmare. I have lost my address book and other files due to a virus. Everything has gone down when I needed an urgent e-mail. I have since discovered that I can go to any computer and get my e-mail at www.mail2web.com. Thank goodness that snail mail or using the telephone are always options.

As time goes by, I continuously discover ways of enriching my relationship with my computer and making it easier to use. Some involve personal comfort. I am kind to my body. I keep a tube of topical cream for muscle aches beside the computer. I sometimes wear a wrist support. I place soft pillows behind my back and under my seat. After all, there is no one at home to massage my muscles on demand. I must relax them by myself. My cats are always ready to receive a rubdown. This does soothe my hands.

Overall, I find that I enjoy the benefits of my computer every day and night. As I discover the amazing number of places to visit on the Internet, I feel fortunate to have this machine with all of its options despite the occasional frustrations and challenges.

So, Can You, Should You, Might You or Will You?!?!

Checklist of Choices

☐ Keep all instruction manuals for the computer, printer and scanner. Read them often. Post the phone number for the help-line by the telephone.

☐ Make several friends who are computer geeks. This can add to your social life, save you money and prevent trips to a service depot.

- [ ] Know one computer repairman who will make house calls. This can be expensive but worth it if your back gives out when you carry machinery that weighs over two ounces.

- [ ] Save important material like your address book, investment portfolio and novel in process on a CD. Power failures occur.

- [ ] Install an anti-virus program. Also keep Aspirin and Tylenol handy for unexpected events like infections and power failures.

- [ ] Fill ink cartridges very slowly and carefully. Or throw away your old cartridge and buy a new one. Saving your sanity is more important than saving money.

- [ ] Send e-mails to keep in touch with friends who live in China, Tanzania and around the corner. You can also talk with strangers in chat rooms.

- [ ] Look up jokes, cartoons and quotations for a daily laugh or an inspirational thought. You can be your own best friend and entertain yourself when you are at home alone.

- [ ] Subscribe to newsletters for daily company. For example, there are ones for dieters, animal lovers and positive thinkers.

- [ ] Connect to your public library. Great service is there for you. You can browse the catalogue and reserve your books in advance of your personal visit. Also, see the home pages for links to events, book reviews and news.

- [ ] Play games at midnight or later when you have the blues. Try Scrabble, solitaire or poker.

- [ ] Add a Blackberry to your life. Connect with others at any time and from any place.

PART 6

ON SEARCHING FOR MR. OR MS. RIGHT

Even though I am surviving and thriving as a single person, the quest for a partner still tickles my fancy from time to time. I have read *Cats Are Better Than Men*. Many times! But, cats cannot take me out for dinner and a movie. They are not the greatest traveling companions, meowing all the way to any destination when we go by car. So, I remain open to the possibility of meeting my soul mate.

I am in my sixties, yet hope continues to reside in my heart. I know that older men often have difficulty with their backs and other physical organs; but, that is okay. A younger man would be acceptable. In her book *The Joys of Aging...and How to Avoid Them*, Phyllis Diller argues that "the only men who are too young are the ones who write their love letters in crayon, wear pajamas with feet, or fly for half-fare."

I dream of a gentleman who would be the light of my life. Since I am happy with myself and my life, he would be the icing on my cake. The challenge is to find someone who wants a committed long-term relationship with me and my felines instead of a short-term sexual conquest.

He must like sharing some of his time and interests and desire occasional trips together. He has to drive and be able to carry groceries. Qualities like humor, sensitivity, kindness and honesty are essential. A full head of hair would also be nice.

You might want to spice up and add warmth to your life with a friend, companion, lover or mate. We all deserve our just desserts. A sweet treat is lovely after a good meal and icing does add flavor to a cake. Brace yourself for the challenges and pursue the opportunities of this quest in the twenty-first century.

1. FINDING SEX PLUS

I have found that many men have mainly sex on their minds. Sex-hungry men can be found anywhere. He may be the charming gentleman that you meet at the market or a dashing dance partner at a party. However, caution is important when talking to strangers. Sociopaths and psychopaths also shop for groceries and attend parties. I offer my smiles only to the cashier when shopping. I know that they are bonded and will avoid sexual harassment to avoid a trial by jury.

Some planning is necessary to block partners who are just looking for a fast and frivolous fling. First and foremost, I look for a man who wants to be in my company for awhile. The R and C words—relationship and commitment—are not alien to his vocabulary. Second, I have long lists of desired traits for the partner of my dreams and rules to guide my hunting. For example, he must love cats, reading and movies. Third, he will bring me Belgian chocolates, white roses and sparkling wine for candlelight chats. Selecting the right places and times to connect with Mr. Right is like a jigsaw puzzle.

I wonder what are the best ways to meet someone in order to encourage the right pieces of a relationship to fit together. Once, I thought I had found my perfect partner when I was at home alone. I received a telephone call from an employee of a dating service that I did not join after attending the initial interview. I took a risk and met this gentleman. The sparks flew on our first date. However, our days together were numbered as he was not totally available. He was legally separated and the divorce process took its toll on our budding relationship.

I prefer to date only men that I meet through a friend or relative or at the office of my veterinarian. If we get together for a first date in a restaurant for lunch when the sun shines brightly, I can at least enjoy a meal, if not his company; I will also be able to see what he looks like. I try to avoid meeting men in a dim bar with loud music; low visibility and blaring sounds make it impossible to see my date and clearly hear his voice, leading to distorted impressions.

Knowing when I am ready to hunt for a man and planning before taking action is important. I create an outline of the man of my dreams and devise a strategy to find him. This process can fill many evenings when I am at home alone. Devising test questions as "Are you married?" or "Do you love cats?" are essential to protect myself from being swept away by chemistry and infatuation. I know that I want my passion as part of a committed relationship.

So, Can You, Should You, Might You or Will You?!?!

Checklist of Choices

☐ Hug and caress yourself. You want to perfect these skills before handling a real person. This can also prevent starvation for the warmth of human touch, that could lead to only sex rather than a loving relationship.

☐ Treat yourself to touching experiences. Try massage, a pedicure and hugging a friend or your pet unless it is a fish.

- Ladies, take seven friends to the singles' dance. Chances of all of them connecting with someone is rare. So, you will have a person to go home with rather than accepting a lift with the first man who touches you.

- Take a cold shower and play some squash before your first few dates. Slow down your sexual desires so you can get to know the other person.

- Wear soft colors on a first date. Bright red can excite passions and blind your judgment about your compatibility. Don't shave your legs (ladies) or your face (gentlemen) until after a few dates.

- Require several dates before touching. Have your first kiss outside your home instead of on top of your bed. If he or she wants instant sex, they will fail this test.

- [ ] Visualize the man or woman of your dreams. Create a collage with pictures of diamond rings, couples embracing and strolling by the ocean under a full moon.

- [ ] Believe in your mental powers to attract what you want—sex as part of a committed relationship. Also ask angels and the Divine One for assistance in your quest.

2. ELIMINATING MR. OR MS. WRONG

Part of finding a meaningful relationship is having the wisdom to avoid partners that are wrong for you. In my youth, I was often a smart woman who made foolish choices. I easily got swept away by passion or failed to communicate my needs and desires; thus, I was led astray to connect with unsuitable men. Listening for my partner's goals was not my sharpest skill. It was as if I wore blinkers when it came to examining whether or not our lifestyles, interests and dreams fit together.

I spent many years with a man who was legally separated and willing to commit to me. However, his wife refused to agree to a divorce. The stress of dealing with her moods took its toll on our relationship. I got involved with another separated man whose wife threatened suicide when he asked for a divorce. I ended that partnership. I could not risk the guilt in case she made good on her threat. I now strive to go for the cherries rather than the pits and avoid relationships that are unsuitable or destructive. Four ideas light my path.

First, I cultivate self-love on a daily basis. I smile at myself in the mirror and tell myself what a great catch I am. When I treat myself well, I know that I attract others who treat me well. For example, men who bring a rose to a first date and ask me lots of questions about myself tickle my fancy.

Second, I believe that self-knowledge is essential. What do I require most of all? What would I give up for the man of my dreams? He must love me for myself and accept me as I am. He must love cats, movies and books. He must drive a car rather than a motorcycle. He must use shampoo that banishes dandruff. If we decide to live together or marry, I know that I could not live in a tent or reside with someone who breeds snakes. I could not give up my love of reading, staying up late and sleeping in or living in a building without a swimming pool.

Third, I have learned that it is important to communicate my goals. For example, I got tangled in a relationship with a man who wanted a stepmother for his children while I dreamed of a romantic and passionate liaison. His preferred vacation was Disneyland. I craved a cruise to Hawaii. His children called at all hours in the days before telephone answering machines. I realized things would not work before it was too late.

Fourth, I insist upon honesty. I once dated a man who claimed he was a social worker. He was cute and charming. We spent hours discussing local clinics and methods of psychotherapy. In fact, he was a clerk in a government office.

Finally, I believe that it is important to pay attention to a potential partner's marital status. He or she may be single, separated, divorced or widowed—even still married. Each lifestyle presents unique challenges and conditions. Know your preferences and limits. For example, three children under the age of five and two dogs would tax my energy. A man who lives with his mother would be too threatening for me if he had to constantly choose between meeting her needs or mine. A recent widower can be risky unless he has finished his grieving and moved on with his life.

So, in order to avoid ridiculous or dangerous encounters, proceed with care and caution. Also carry money for a taxi and your brother's phone number in case a quick getaway is required on a first date!

So, Can You, Should You, Might You or Will You?!?!

Checklist of Choices

☐ Know what you want in a partner. Carry a checklist of your desires and dreams. Tatoo it inside your hand in case you lose your list.

☐ Know what you can't stand in a partner. If you are a vegetarian and he loves meat every day, you might become ill in his kitchen.

☐ Bring friends along on a first date. They can sit at the next table at a restaurant and take notes. Feedback from caring people can help you to make wise decisions.

- [ ] Check out the facts of your partner's life. Call him or her at work. Pay a surprise visit around the lunch or dinner hour.

- [ ] When considering a single man over 50 who has never been married, ask him to share his feelings about commitment. Does he still live with his mother?

- [ ] When dating a legally separated man or woman, examine the separation papers and consult your lawyer if you have any questions. He may be separated only for the weekend.

- [ ] Avoid a married man or woman. This can be good for you only if you prefer to be alone on weekends, holidays and special occasions like your birthday.

- [ ] Be open to a relationship with a divorced man or woman without children. However, run if his anger flows throughout your conversation. Also ask about alimony payments and where the ex-spouse lives.

- [ ] Take a chance on a divorced man or woman with children. Yet, be prepared to play baseball on Saturdays followed by dinner at McDonald's. If you also have children on weekends, make sure that one of you drives a van.

- [ ] Win with a widow or widower. Discover if your partner is still carrying a torch for the deceased spouse. Are all of the walls of her or his home covered with photographs of the dead one? Is he or she still wearing a wedding band ten years after the funeral?

- [ ] Take courses on dating, flirting, dressing for success and tantric sex. You might meet someone with a common interest. In addition, the teacher could help you to verify the the student's age, occupation, address and phone number.

- [ ] Always be on the alert for a partner who is smart, honest, funny and kind, who scores zero on your "can't stand list." Write their name in ink in you telephone book as soon as they say "I Love You."

3. ADDING TECHNOLOGY TO YOUR QUEST

I have tried many Internet dating and matching services over the years, especially in winter. It is more comfortable to surf the Internet than drive through the snow to a party. I can sit in front of the screen in flannel pajamas rather than tackling dressing up, putting on make-up and doing my nails. Standing at a dance or a bar is hard on the feet when I wear high heels and my comfortable sneakers do not match my party dresses.

However, success so far has come to me only in the form of pen pals and occasional dates. I once sent e-mails to my "perfect match" for almost a year. We had similar beliefs, values and interests. However, he lived in Las Vegas. When I thought about sacrificing most of my Canadian pension dollars due to the United States exchange rates, my passion dissolved.

I confess that a photograph has often captured my attention and led me to contact a potential partner before closely reading his profile. I responded to an extremely handsome fellow. We exchanged e-mails and then spoke on the telephone. However, when we met, it was a disappointment as there was neither chemistry nor interest in each other. He was a recent widower and still missing his deceased spouse.

I have learned that written descriptions can be misleading. "A few extra pounds" can mean obese rather than pleasantly plump. An interest in walking can refer to strolling from the house to the car. A love of reading can mean that a person reads the sports page, the comics in the newspaper and *TV Guide* to keep informed.

I am wary of free winks offered by some sites. Here you can browse and flirt for free without paying to join a dating service. After about 15 winks back and forth with a gentleman, I finally joined a service in order to respond to his ardor with an e-mail. When we met in person, I found that winking was his best skill rather than conversation. I am now careful about where I click my mouse.

You can also turn towards technology to help you with ending a relationship. One service allows you, for a fee, to click and end your relationship, avoiding an awkward "breakup" conversation. This service will send your ex a plush monkey plus a certificate with his or her name and the official time and date of the breakup.

A follow-up phone call from the service will ensure that the person understands the meaning of the monkey.

So, Can You, Should You, Might You or Will You?!?!

Checklist of Choices

☐ Save your energy and be selective about the dating services you join on the Internet. Choose sites that limit the candidates for your affection. There are ones for Jews, Christians, seniors, vegetarians and animal lovers.

☐ Beware of a 60-year old who wants to meet dates from 20 to 35 years of age. Such characters usually apologize for their age and stress how they look and feel younger.

☐ Ask about the date of a photo. You will then avoid meeting a bald man with arthritis who presents a picture of himself with a full head of hair and playing golf as a teen-ager.

☐ Limit the number of your e-mails. Some people prefer cyber dates and virtual sex. If this is your preferred form of intimacy, you can e-mail each other forever.

☐ Check out an area code before you telephone. If you live in New York and he or she resides in Tahiti, your bill will surprise you.

☐ Dress up before calling if you plan to converse by video phone. Place your telephone in a clean and beautiful part of your home to add ambiance to the conversation.

- [ ] Choose a public place for your first encounter in real life. A restaurant is a good place. You can at least have a dessert even if he or she is not as sweet as you expected.

- [ ] Reconsider seeking liaisons in real life at such places as bars, dances and the office of your vet. Also continue to reply to ads but take a course in handwriting analysis before responding.

4. SEEKING SAFE SEX

I prefer sleeping with cuddly cats and plump pillows to indulging in casual sex with a man that I don't know very well. My days of wild sexual freedom are over since there are so many sexually transmitted diseases that one can catch. On the one hand, there are afflictions like herpes that can be treated and managed. On the other hand, there are diseases like AIDS that can be a killer. Drug-users are definitely on my banned list of potential suitors.

I blush when I have to face these issues in real life with a possible sexual partner. How do you ask about a person's sexual history? How much of my past do I wish to share? Wouldn't it be nice if everyone had to carry papers? Along with our driver's license, we would have an up-to-date form declaring our freedom from AIDS and herpes. This could include a doctor's note plus a government stamp of approval. It is important to remember the names and faces of past partners. The Ministry of Health and police may have them on their hit list.

So, to be on the safe side, condoms are essential. I know that I can select any number of types such as: glow-in-dark, colored or neutral, latex or animal skin, ribbed or plain, and lubricated or dry. I pray that the cashier does not shout into the microphone: "price check for Lady's Trojans twelve-pack." Still, I feel strongly that no one is worth risking death or a painful disease. Thus, I make sure that reason rules my desires when making choices in this area of a relationship.

So, Can You, Should You, Might You or Will You?!?!

Checklist of Choices

☐ Start dating in junior high school. If you are both each other's first lovers, you should be safe—unless he or she is on heroin and shares needles with friends.

☐ Get to know someone well before sexual contact begins. At least, you will know your partner's recent history, hoping they share the truth with you.

☐ Go for a blood test to check for HIV at your local clinic before or after all coffee, dinner and movie dates when sexual desire is burning. View this as a sexy prelude to more intimate forms of contact.

- Buy your condoms at midnight. Line-ups are short. You will probably not meet your mother at the drug store at that hour.

- Save sex for after marriage You will know where your partner spends his or her nights. The days may still be a mystery unless they work at home.

- Limit physical contact to chaste pecks on the cheek, shoulders or fingertips. Don't drool saliva. Watch out for open cuts.

- Go virtual for all your sexual urges and needs. Join chat groups and e-mail your lovers. Telephone sex is also acceptable. Expect some side effects such as tender wrists, a sore neck and tired eyes.

- Try massages and celibacy instead of sex. This can be much cheaper than dating and so relaxing. You will only have to cope with such ailments as a cold or the flu.

PART 7

READING TREASURES

As a book-lover and a retired librarian, I can not imagine a day or evening without reading. I have a favorite bookmark with a cartoon figure reading a book; there is the caption at the bottom that says "YOU ALWAYS HAVE A FRIEND". As long as I have books in my home and am able to read, loneliness can be held at bay and transformed into a delightful and enriching experience with an absorbing novel or uplifting self-help book. My cats also love books, in their own way. They like to rub their heads against the edges when I am deeply involved with reading, trying to keep my book closed for a good sniff rather than open for my convenience.

Here is an annotated reading list. The selection represents books that have informed, inspired and entertained me as I learned how to survive and thrive solo. The titles were recommended by friends and acquaintances, discovered by chance or selected because they received good reviews. I hope that many will speak to you, teach you new skills and add sparkles to your journey.

The annotations are arranged in response to seven questions that you might ask when you live alone. There are general self-help books about being single that cover many areas and ones that focus on specific topics like cooking for one or coping with major life changes (such as loss of a love, divorce, aging and becoming a widow or widower). Other books listed here can help you to explore meaningful ways to enjoy solitude, avenues of creativity and the possibility of pet ownership (in other words, being owned by a pet). There are also books listed that can guide you if you wish to seek a partner (or not).

How Can I Survive & Thrive on My Own?

The Art of Living Single.

By Michael Broder.

New York: Avon Books, 1988.

Dr. Broder is a clinical psychologist and pioneer in research and counseling for divorce and transition adjustment. He presents a set of tools for shaping a life as a single person. The book was written to share the experiences of people living on their own and to help you to listen to your own voice.

He emphasizes the importance of liking yourself and valuing your time alone as one of your most treasured possessions. As you learn what you want, you can become empowered to choose the life you desire and acquire skills in the art of living.

There are chapters on strategies for dealing with people, handling loneliness and seeking romance. Dr. Broder's sections on romantic strategies cover all aspects of such relationships from testing your desire for this type of partner, becoming involved and maintaining the bond to dealing with the pain of breaking up. Finally, there is a section on survival strategies which covers where and how you live and work, balancing work and play, security issues, medical concerns and finance.

Throughout, Dr. Broder suggests that you make inventories of your attitudes in order to understand your goals. By identifying options, you can control your future and choose activities you enjoy. The wealth of stories told by single people in varied circumstances brings the material to life.

I have found that creating inventories related to my goals has kept me on track to enjoy my single lifestyle. For example, when I wanted more social contact, I listed friends and acquaintances whom I could call, clubs I might join and courses I considered taking. Throwing the occasional party also helped me to feel connected and reduced my feeling of isolation. In addition I became motivated to do some intensive housework and clean up my home; I keep the floors clean for my felines, but tend to leave dusting until I have company.

Chicken Soup for the Single's Soul: Stories of Love and Inspiration for the Single, Divorce and Widowed.

By Jack Canfield, Mark Victor Hansen et al.
Deerfield Beach, Florida: Health Communications, Inc., 1999.
Single people in varied circumstances tell stories about the tough times and unique joys of being single. Adults who are single, divorced, widowed or single parents share their experiences of making their own lives fulfilling and enriching the lives of others.

The stories are arranged under the following headings:
SINGLE AND HAPPY; DATING; FINDING YOUR MATE;
MAKING A DIFFERENCE; SINGLE PARENTING;
SINGLE AGAIN; LOSING A PARTNER; and WE ARE NOT ALONE.

One bachelor tells how he became single and happy; after years of searching for his soul mate, he learned that it was himself. A single woman replaced the frenzy of family holiday dinners at Christmas without a partner with serving meals at a shelter for the homeless; she went on to do other volunteer work, finding that caring for others filled a void in her life. Joan Rivers discusses dating again after the suicide of her husband. She honestly tells of her awkwardness and disappointments as she eased back into the world of searching for romance. A woman who was divorced and widowed became a light in darkness for others by creating greeting cards for people going through a divorce ("Ex's & Oh's"). A widow with no children ran a corner candy store and mothered her whole community by her involvement with the people around her.

Both the challenges and the rewards of being on one's own are presented in the stories. Inspiring quotations and delightful cartoons add to the enjoyment of reading this book. You are bound to find stories that speak to your circumstances and concerns.

When I read about people in the same boat as myself, I feel comforted and I can accept my lifestyle. I see it as an exciting choice and value my freedom and independence.

Living Alone & Loving It: A Guide to Relishing the Solo Life.

By Barbara Feldon.

New York: Simon & Schuster, 2003.

I love this book for its focus upon the rewarding, uplifting and positive aspects of living alone. Feldon emphasizes that a successful single
celebrates life and lives with curiosity and enthusiasm. We are entre-
preneurs of our destiny and happiness is in our own hands.

The author discusses basic areas such as handling finances, defining
our interests, connecting with other and travelling solo. She offers
practical tips for banishing negative thinking and ways to connect
with others in times of crisis. It is important to stop believing that
marriage is the solution to loneliness and the only road to happiness.

Feldon reminds us that one delight of living alone is the freedom
to arrange and decorate our living spaces to suit our whims and desires. Our homes can be a sanctuary, filled with things we love. There
is no one around to dictate our tastes. Sharing our places with people
we like is highly recommended.

When we do not have a loving, romantic relationship in our lives,
friendships are important to avoid destructive infatuations. The author
suggests that sensual experiences are constantly available and can
provide pleasure when a sexual partner is absent.

The crown jewel of solitude is described as the gift of time to
develop our creativity in a play space where we can serve our muse.
When we are creative, it is possible to dive into realms that are
deeper and more complete than our surface lives. Activities such
as painting, writing or sculpting can greatly enhance the quality of
our lives.

Barbara Feldon was Agent "99" on the television series *Get Smart*.
She is a feminist, activist and lecturer. Her book covers both emotional
and practical aspects of living and is written in an accessible style.

Whenever, I feel the slightest bit lonely or blue, I read this book and am inspired to focus inwards to develop my coping skills and to reach outwards to connect with new people and activities. I always find ways to feel both grateful and excited about my life. I see that there are so many little ways to celebrate and enjoy being on my own. I can sip wine by candlelight and dine in front to the television at 10 p.m. without having to dress up for another person. I can snuggle under the covers in my bed and finish my novel at 2 a.m. and then sleep until noon. Or I can paint until the sun rises, leaving all my supplies lying about until the next day.

Single: The Art of Being Satisfied, Fulfilled and Independent.
By Judy Ford.
Avon, Massachusetts: Adams Media, 2004.

Judy Ford is a psychotherapist and writer who has experienced widowhood, divorce and single parenting. She offers a celebration of living alone that draws upon her own life.

The material is presented in an inspiring and practical manner. The book begins with a list of 52 things that a satisfied single knows. Examples are the importance of being kind to yourself, bonding with others and self-acceptance. Life is too short to spend it yearning for what we don't have. The author shows ways to have a wonderful life, love ourselves and deal with challenges. Throughout the book, there are sections called "Try This" with concrete suggestions like planning for lonely times, having a daily spiritual practice and baking heart-shaped cookies for yourself and others. Creativity is seen as a great healer and we are encouraged to jump into our passion.

This is one of the best surveys of life on one's own since it deals with all aspects of the single life in a personal, practical and uplifting way. Quotations are scattered throughout the work. The final one is by Oscar Wilde. "To love oneself is the beginning of a life-long romance." I often ponder these words of wisdom when romance is absent from my life or my sense of self worth and desirability need a boost.

The Battersea Park Road to Enlightenment.
By Isabel Losada.
London: Bloomsbury Publishing, 2001.
Isabel is a divorced lady, a Starbucks addict and a person allergic to exercise. She set out on a path to self awareness and enlightenment in order to be happy every day. Isabel visited nuns in a convent, astrologers and various types of massage therapists. She took workshops on tantric sex, releasing anger, Tai Chi and being born again. She also explored rolfing, colonic irrigation, pathways to manifesting the inner goddess and dealing with co-dependency.

I have found it is necessary to know myself in order to find meaningful ways to cope and grow. Trying new activities is a challenge, with no one urging me to do so. I do not want the couch, the television and the refrigerator to be my best friends.

This book gave me a wealth of ideas for exploring new ways to grow and enrich my life. Losada includes lists of books and contacts (American and British) for each phase of her journey. She is an author, a singer, dancer and television producer who lives in Battersea in London, England. Losada writes with great honesty and wit and displays a serious commitment to her growth, bound to inspire you to explore new horizons.

Living Alone & Liking It!: a complete guide to living on your own.

By Lynn Shahan.

New York: HarperCollins, 1984.

Lynne Shahan presents a very positive attitude towards living alone.
She stresses the following: the opportunities for exploration, the
chances for personal fulfillment, the value of unlimited freedom;
the rewards of new experiences, and the time to get to know yourself.

On the one hand, the author is sympathetic to the stressful aspects
of adjusting to living alone, especially if this occurs due to divorce
or the loss of a spouse. She takes you through the beginning period
as you deal with grief until acceptance and self-reliance can emerge.
Shahan emphasizes that living alone can be a mixture of feelings of
joy and excitement and emotions like fear and anxiety. Acceptance is
a key factor in creating a satisfying life. There is an excellent chapter
on combating loneliness and transforming it into a comfortable state
of aloneness. Many concrete suggestions are given, such as developing interests that do not require another person.

On the other hand, Shahan emphasizes the positive aspects of
living alone. We are responsible for making our own fun by entertaining ourselves and others, pursuing hobbies and going places alone
to encounter new people and adventures.

Finally, the book covers practical aspects of living alone. There are
sections on cooking (including recipes), choosing where one lives
(for safety and convenience) and planning for financial security.

This book is easy to read. I consult it often. I always find remind-
ers that I don't have to be lonely when I am alone. Rather, there are
sources of pleasure to be found in my privacy and solitude. I also like
the fact that Shahan discusses both the happy and stressful aspects of

living alone. So, I do not feel guilty when loneliness or apathy overwhelms me at times.

What Can I Cook for Myself?

Cooking for One. *By Better Homes and Gardens.*
Des Moines, Iowa, Meredith Corporation, 1987.
Here is a basic book for you when new to cooking for one.
There are brief instructions on shopping, equipping your kitchen and storing foods. The book is arranged into sections on: morning meals (often omitted in cookbooks), light meals of sandwiches, soups and salads, main meals (fish, chicken and meat using a variety of cooking methods as stir-fry, roasting and poaching), and the rest of the meal (soups, sauces and desserts). The text is easy to follow. Beautiful photographs illustrate each finished dish. There are not too many dishes in each section; so, you will not be overwhelmed at any stage of creating a meal only for yourself.

Solo Suppers: Simple Delicious Meals to Cook for Yourself.
By Joyce Goldstein.
San Francisco: Chronicle Books, 2003.
This book is intended for those who love good food and see cooking as a rewarding and creative activity. You need some leisure time to create these dishes. A detailed introduction prepares you for shopping for one, planning meals and stocking your kitchen. The author focuses upon the evening meal since this is the one that can have the most impact, especially if you work full-time. Exquisite colored photographs are given for each recipe. There are sections on sauces, soups, salads, pastas and grains, eggs and cheese, fish and seafood, poultry and meat plus desserts. You will find fascinating combinations of ingredients such as duck and Belgian endive salad with pear and seafood curry with coconut, citrus and cucumber. Here is a great guide for the adventurous chef.

The 15-Minute Single Gourmet: 100 Deliciously Simple Recipes For One. *By Paulette Mitchell.*
New York: Macmillan, 1994.
Paulette Mitchell created this cookbook to offer an antidote to junk food and monotony for everyone from college students to busy workers or retirees. She presents an enticing variety of recipes for pasta, ethnic and vegetarian dishes, soups, fish, chicken, salads and desserts. This book is noteworthy for its focus upon health. The author gives nutritional information for each dish—calories with the amount from fat, protein, carbohydrates and cholesterol. There are also excellent tips for selecting your ingredients as you shop and a detailed index. With this book, you can treat yourself to simple yet tasty, nutritious and interesting meals.

Frugal Feasts: 101 Quick & Easy Single-Serving Meals from Around the World.

By Mary Spilsbury Ross.

New York: Doubleday, 1996.

The author presents recipes consisting of inexpensive foods like rice, pasta and beans. The dishes can be made by new or experienced chefs with minimal preparation and cooked in less than 20 minutes. Within each chapter on foods such as salads or pasta, there are selections of classic dishes from a variety of countries. You can consult the index to find all the dishes from Russia, Canada or Italy or all of the recipes using rice or beans. Also included are useful herb and spice mixtures plus a list of basic kitchen equipment. You might fancy a Caribbean pumpkin soup from St. Lucia, chicken with peanut sauce from Indonesia or pasta with walnuts from Italy. This cookbook will satisfy your desire for some adventure in the kitchen. It is also a practical resource for those with a limited budget.

Starting Out: The Essential Guide to Cooking on Your Own.

By Julie Van Rosendaal

Vancouver: Whitecap, 2006

Van Rosendaal tells you everything you need to know about cooking. The book covers basics like buying gadgets and appliances and stocking the pantry, and includes recipes for every category of food such as salads, beans, beef and cakes. There are suggestions for leftovers included wiht every recipe. A chapter on produce gives lists of fruits and vegetables with information on when each is in season, shopping advice and methods of storage and preparation.

Charming illustrations are sprikled throughout the text. The author's chapter on "Tips From Mom" provides useful tidbits, like determining if an egg is fresh (it will sink in a pan of cool water) and softening hard brown sugar (by placing it in a dish with a slice of apple or bread, covering it and putting it in the microwave for a few seconds). This book would be excellent for the novice chef and useful for experienced cooks.

What are Ways to Handle Change?

Dave Barry Turns 50.

By Dave Barry.

New York: Ballantine Books, 1999.

If you are living on your own as a divorced person or widow or widower, you might be tackling many tasks for the first time, such as creating a budget or buying a new car. If you are single by choice, you always face challenges like travelling on your own or coping with loneliness. Changes are constant in life, in relation to people, places and objects.

Getting older is one change that we all must face. Finding your sense of humor can be your greatest discovery to help you to deal with the changes. After I read a humorous book, I can adopt a lighter attitude and view my wrinkles, wider waistline and sagging flesh on my upper arms with more acceptance. I sink into a state of high anxiety when I picture myself old and sick and alone. If I read something funny, I am able to get a handle on my mood and carry on.

Whatever your age, Dave Barry's book offers you a hilarious look at the aging process. The author shares his memories of major political events, music, fads and trends. He mentions such varied events as the Bomb, hula hoops, Elvis Presley, the Kennedy assassination, the Beatles, the Vietnam protests and Watergate.

I particularly enjoyed Mr. Barry's account of his difficulty accepting the need for reading glasses. He often preferred to forget or lose them. So, he would find himself at a restaurant ordering from the blurry blurbs on the menu and selecting "We do not accept personal checks." Deciding upon his order by reading from the menu of a person at a distant table was also an option for him as he could read items far away. I recall my own experience of adjusting to reading glasses, especially when walking down stairs and could relate to his anecdotes.

Barry's book is bound to elicit many smiles, chuckles and loud laughs as you read about his experiences, beliefs and desires. Focusing upon the lighter side of serious concerns about getting older can definitely help us to survive and thrive as we face inevitable changes.

How to Survive the Loss of a Love: 58 Things To Do When There Is Nothing to Be Done.

By Harold Bloomfield, Melba Colgrove and Peter McWilliams.

New York: Bantam Books, 1993. Revised paperback trade edition.

This is a beautiful and sensitive book about coping with the loss of a loving relationship whether through a break-up, divorce or death. The authors are a psychologist (Colgrove), a psychiatrist (Bloomfield) and a poet (McWilliams). They guide you though surviving, healing and growing again amidst all of the changes encountered after we lose an important person in our lives. The book offers concrete ways to survive. There is an emphasis upon accepting your loss, keeping decision-making to a minimum, giving yourself comfort and social support and surrounding yourself with living things like plants or pets.

The authors explore three phases of healing: shock/denial, anger/depression, and understanding/acceptance. You are advised to take steps like proceeding at your own pace, pampering yourself, eating well and keeping a journal. It is important to avoid rekindling the old relationship or entering a new one on the rebound. An emotional wound deserves respect and gentleness.

Finally, you are asked to believe that you will grow again. The following steps are suggested: forgiving the old partner after a break-up, opening to new people, discovering your creativity, finding the joys of solitude, and enjoying the freedom and opportunities that are available to you on your own. This book is like a security blanket that can be used for warmth as you adjust to being alone again after the loss of a significant relationship. The following quotes express the essence of the journey after a relationship ends due to divorce or breaking up with a lover. "I loved... which was purgatory. I lost... which was hell. And I survived...Heaven!" I have turned towards this book again and again as I lost lovers, friends and parents. The prose is so exquisite and the practical tips for coping are offered in such a gentle and loving manner.

Who Moved My Cheese: An Amazing Way to Deal with Change in Your Work and in Your Life.

By Spencer Johnson.

New York: G. P. Putnam's Sons, 1998.

This book tells the story about four imaginary characters who live in a maze and survive on cheese, representing what we want to have in life and different ways of reacting to change. Sniff and Scurry are mice and Hem and Haw are little people. When the characters are confronted with the loss of cheese in the usual places, they display a range of different reactions such as sniffing out change when it happens, scurrying into action, being afraid, denying and resisting change or learning to adapt. The book is illustrated throughout with drawings of wedges of cheese and sayings like "The quicker you let go of old cheese the sooner you find new cheese."

The author is a medical doctor who also has a B.A. in Psychology. He writes with exceptional clarity and simplicity, reducing complex ideas into easy, practical guides for action. This is a book that you can read in about an hour and learn the essential tools for coping with unexpected, unplanned or planned changes in any area of your life.

I have turned to this book when facing major lifestyle changes such as retirement or minor changes like buying a new chair. I easily found ways to release old patterns of behavior, outdated beliefs or attachments to objects. Then, I could open myself to new opportunities.

Men on Divorce: The Other Side of the Story.

By Penny Kaganoff & Susan Spano (eds).

New York: Harcourt Brace & Company, 1997.

Fifteen American writers of different cultural and ethnic back-
grounds discuss their divorces. The aim of the book is to help those
who are divorced or going through the process to understand
themselves; it is also intended for people watching someone
they care about face a divorce.

All of the stories are deeply touching. The men openly share
the anguish of their divorces and the stress they experienced before
finding the strength, stamina and resilience to survive and thrive
again. For example, Ted Sototaroff describes his guilt and grief as
he mourned and learned how to atone. He encountered anger,
blame and loneliness until he finally learned to live alone and
become self-sufficient. Yoga, meditation, valium and a kitten
helped him through the changes in his life.

In another story, Edward Hoagland, a black veteran, chose to
leave his life and family in order to become a writer. He emphasized
the guilt he experienced over the years until he finally divorced 12
years after his separation.

Another divorced man, Michael Ryan, offers a humorous take by
writing a practical guide on how to get divorced. He advises men
to speak up whenever nagged by their wives about such things as:
physical flaws, having too much fun, reading the newspaper at meals
rather than talking, holding grudges, and being selfish. In addition,
requesting sex crudely and refusing it when offered can do the trick
to encourage divorce.

I read this book to better understand the divorced men in my life.
I emerged with much empathy for the physical, mental, social and

emotional changes divorced men must face before they can commit
to relationships again.

Beginnings: A book for Widows.

By Betty Jane Wylie.

Toronto: McClelland & Stewart, 1977. 4th revised edition.

If you select only one book on surviving and thriving as a widow,
choose this one. Betty Jane Wylie compassionately discusses the
ups and downs of adjusting to being a widow and offers practical
ways to meet new beginnings. She writes from her own experience.
In 1973, Wylie suddenly lost her husband due to his asphyxiation
from food that got stuck in his windpipe. She had four children
to raise. The author was a published poet and playwright who was
able to turn towards journalism and non-fiction, writing over 30
books since her husband's death. Her style is straightforward, with
an emphasis on facing facts and opening to opportunities.

There are chapters on handling emotions after the death of a
spouse, like depression and anger. She gently guides you through
stages of mourning and presents options like using an electric blanket
for warmth or joining a self-help group. Wylie then discusses all aspects of the jolt of living alone after marriage such as having to shape
new routines, cooking meals only for yourself and enjoying yourself
without the deceased spouse. Her chapter on finances is partly
Canadian and partly American in content, including an excellent
list of money-saving tips, relevant wherever you live. Other issues
that are unique to widows are helping children to cope, dealing with
the maintenance of one's home and handling the possessions of your
late husband.

Finally, the author gives many suggestions related to social life. There is a sensitive discussion on socializing and reacting to other people as they respond to your new status. There is advice for those seeking romantic relationships again and advice about the variety of other relations available to you (friends, family or involvement in a cause outside yourself). Wylie describes "happy lists" you can create such as writing down destinations for future trips, treats to buy for yourself and menus for dinner parties.

Although I am not a widow, after reading Wylie's book I learned how to empathize deeply with the widows that I know and relate to them with sensitivity. I am more aware of the depth of their mourning and the strength they must discover in order to build a new lifestyle.

How Can I Enjoy My Time Alone?

Positive Solitude: a Practical Program for Mastering Loneliness And Achieving Self-Fulfillment.

By Rae Andre.

New York: HaperCollins, 1991.

Rae Andre turned towards her lifelong friends in order to write this book—authors of popular and academic books, people who wrote personal stories and researchers. There are references to people such as Henry David Thoreau, Victor Frankl, May Sarton and Abraham Maslow. She addresses people facing loneliness plus persons who enjoy being alone most of the time but want to get more out of their solitude.

Andre suggests that we can choose to adopt a positive attitude in order to enrich our experience of being alone. Three phases are suggested. First, we have to open ourselves to solitude and learn to provide our own feedback as to what is satisfying. Second, we can change as we recognize our needs and priorities, knowing what gives us meaningful and pleasurable feedback. Third, we can engage in exploration, to develop our creativity, spirituality or whatever empowers us when we are at home alone. There are concrete suggestions for those who are newly alone such as the divorced or widowed and ideas for making decisions in a constructive manner, with the help of others as needed.

Her chapters on sensuality and laughter have influenced my life in positive ways. I am encouraged to nourish my senses. To smell lilacs, perfume and spring air. To listen to birds, music and the water as I shower. To enjoy being touched by going for a massage or hugging my friends. To eat slowly and taste my food and savor my morning coffee. To take the time to look at art, flowers and the colors in my home.

I have also committed myself to smiling and lightening up. I have created a "humor environment" in my home. I place cartoons, jokes, funny mobiles, toys and whimsical objects like a teddy bear around my place. I keep a cartoon by *Ziggy* beside my computer with the caption "The nice thing about being your own best friend…is that you're always around when you need you!!" My cats' toys cover the floors in every room; feathers, ping pong balls and bells can be tossed around for a play session whenever the mood strikes.

As I discover, cultivate and enjoy my skills in handling solitude, I can become centered, contented, sensual and happy. Then, I have more to offer people and my relationships are enriched.

Celebrating Time Alone: Stories of Splendid Solitude.

By Lionel Fisher.

Hillsboro, Oregon: BeyondWords Publishing, Inc., 2001.

Lionel Fisher spent six years by himself on a remote island in the Pacific Northwest. He shares his experiences and reflections to help the reader to find answers to concerns and paths for fulfillment. The author writes about his interviews with people who were alone because significant others in their lives died or went away plus people who chose to be alone. For example, there are stories about hermits who live on an island or in a cabin in the woods and a story from a divorced woman who delights in her freedom to be totally herself and find pleasure in daily activities.

Fisher defines true serenity as closeness to the self. Solitude is viewed as a prize that spending time alone can give us. We can explore our thoughts, fantasies and plans to emerge as authentic people, who give compassion and kindness towards ourselves and others. We are encouraged to engage in just being instead of constant and frantic doing. Fisher believes that it is not being alone that is the cause of loneliness; rather, it is living a self-centered, unloving and friendless life.

I turn to this book whenever my life becomes flooded with activities. After I reading Fisher's eloquent and witty prose, I slow down, relax and take a look at what is truly important to me. His ideas enable me to know and reap the benefits and blessings of my solitude. I can pursue my passions for painting and writing or just take it easy and read as long as I desire.

Loving Yourself: Four Steps to A Happier You.

By Daphne Rose Kingma.

Emeryville, CA: Conari Press, 2004.

Kingma believes that the greatest work we will do in this life is to love ourselves. She hopes that by reading and using this book we can learn to nourish our hearts, bodies, minds and souls.

Would you like to love and accept yourself more but don't know how to do this? The author offers four concrete steps you can take to know and appreciate your unique and precious self. First, express and reveal your feelings and needs. Second, take action and try new things. Third, clear clutter from your mind, closets, environment and relationships. Fourth, approach life with compassion, giving to yourself and others.

Daphne Rose Kingma is a psychotherapist, lecturer, author, workshop leader and teacher of relationships as a spiritual form. Her writing is rich in anecdotes and she uses language in a way that instantly connects you to the people and ideas presented.

All books on living alone successfully emphasize the importance of enjoying our own company and having a loving relationship with ourselves. When I read this book and apply the suggestions, I always clear a bit of clutter from my mind and life, resulting in small acts that cause me to like myself better. It might be shuffling aside self-pity to make a list of things for which I am grateful, cleaning my closet and donating old clothes to the poor or focusing on another person and telephoning a homebound friend.

The Invitation.

By Oriah Mountain Dreamer.

San Francisco: HarperCollins, 1999.

When we live alone, we usually have a lot of time to get to know ourselves and identify what we deeply believe, value and desire. Then we can use our freedom to live according to our wishes. Oriah Mountain Dreamer invites us to live fully and passionately with hope, faith and a deep commitment to ourselves and others. The book is a journey directed towards being fully alive and experiencing every aspect of daily life.

The author poses questions, shares her values and beliefs and helps us to explore our responses to our longings, fears, joys and sources of deep sustenance. At the end of each chapter, there is a meditation exercise. For example, to get in touch with our longings and deepest desires, she tells us how to breathe deeply, relax our bodies and write about our wants, needs and desires to discover what we really want in life.

Oriah Mountain Dreamer is an author and leader of workshops, ceremonies and retreats throughout North America. She writes openly about her life experiences and articulates her dreams and desires with great eloquence. She has been divorced and survived many other relationships as she has moved along to discover where she belongs and the purpose of her life—to study and learn, to teach and to love well. Her delight in both sensuality and spirituality is inspiring.

When I read this book (and do the exercises), I am able to get in touch with what I really want to do with my time alone. I stop frantically looking to others for activities. I am able to relax at home by myself. I enjoy all of my sensual experiences—tasting, touching, smelling, hearing, seeing and take pleasure in daily activities like watering my plants and pursue my hobbies or read a good book.

The Wonders of Solitude.

By Dale Salwak (ed).

The ClassicWisdom Collection.

San Rafael, California: NewWorld Library, 1995.

Here is a collection of inspiring thoughts on solitude from a
wide range of people. There are quotation from poets, novelists,
playwrights, philosophers, psychologists, artists and theologians.
The material is arranged around the following themes: solitude as
discovery (finding self and God), solitude as inspiration (finding
inward peace and creativity), and the power of silence. There is
also a chapter on places to find solitude such as at home, in houses
of worship, among others, and within the human heart.

This work is a gem of a companion for anyone who lives alone and
is seeking meaningful moments and times of quiet contemplation.
I often consult the book in the morning to find food for thought to
take me through the day, especially when I am going to be alone.
The selections are poetic and profound. I always find some nugget
of wisdom to give me some inner peace before I rush into the demands
of my day.

Meditations for Men Who Do Next To Nothing (And Would Like To Do Even Less).

By Lee Ward Shore.

New York: Warner Books, 1994.

This book is for the modern man who wants to eliminate all activity and decision making in order to find serenity. Working harder, faster and more diligently is to be surrendered to inactivity. The book is also intended for women so they can understand the peace that comes from intertia.

Shore presents quotations (only from men), a brief discussion of a personal issue and a reminder to help the reader stay on course. He covers a wide range of issues like quiet time, being in charge and expectations. For example, the issue of "Courage" is introduced by the following quote by Muhammad Ali: "I am the greatest." After comments on this topic, the reader is given the advice to honk if you love yourself. The issue of "Helplessness" begins with an Indian proverb: "Sitting is better than standing, lying is better than sitting." The author suggests that just finding a reason to get up in the morning is enough of a challenge.

After reading any chapter, I am encouraged to accept myself when I feel like doing nothing, just sitting on a chair and gazing at the clouds. I can shove my "to-do" list under my place mat and enjoy being idle for awhile. After all, no one is around to nag me to be productive. Only my cats are present to express their needs and might meow if their food bowls are empty.

Am I Creative?

The Artist's Way: A Spiritual Path to Higher Creativity.

By Julia Cameron.

New York: Putnam Publishing, 1992.

This book unleashed my creativity. I discovered it at a period in my life when I faced difficulties with how to spend my time alone. I had an irregular work schedule with variable shifts. So, I could not join groups or classes that met regularly. Also, I had limited time and energy after coping with work and chores. After following the exercises in the book, I discovered and followed my dreams to write and paint, activities I could pursue at my convenience.

Julia Cameron draws from her rich background as a writer who has created novels, plays, songs and poems plus scripts for television and films. She views creativity as God's gift to us and presents strategies on how to use our creativity as our way of giving back to God. Her writing is clear and full of passion.

The basic tools for exploring and developing our creativity consist of "Morning Pages," daily writing whatever comes to mind for three pages and a weekly "Artist's Date," spending time in solitude with self-nurturing activities, pampering and play. The program is outlined in 12 chapters that focus upon such topics as safety, identity, power, possibility, abundance and connection. There are delightful exercises at the end of each chapter. For example, after the section on recovering a sense of strength, we are guided to connect with our dream and particular form of creativity by repeating affirmations, visualizing our success, listing ways of manifesting our goals and looking for ways to remove blocks. The margins of each page contain wonderful quotations to inspire your journeys.

You might wish to compose music, write poems or novels or create paintings. Your desires could be to cook with flair, form better relationships or improve your self-awareness and self-esteem. The book is a great guide to help you to spend your time alone in meaningful and joyous pursuits. See also Julia Cameron's bestsellers on the creative process such as *Vein of Gold, The Right to Write and Finding Water: The Art of Perseverance*.

Writing Down The Bones: Freeing the Writer Within.

By Natalie Goldberg.

Boston: Shambhala, 1986.

Natalie Goldberg presents a way of writing that can help you to know and express your life experiences and maintain your sanity. She believes that we can find the "essential and awake speech of our minds to express what we want and need to say."

Goldberg gives six rules for writing practice, to be done as timed exercises for ten to 60 minutes. Keep your hand moving. Don't cross anything out. Don't worry about punctuation, spelling or grammar.

Lose control. Don't think and don't get logical. Go for the jugular—i.e., flow with scary or emotionally charged feelings.

Goldberg suggests many topics for this free style of writing such as a color, streets in your city, a meal you love or memories of your first sexual experience. There are also basic tips like using concrete and specific terms (e.g., saying pansy rather than flower), showing rather than telling and eventually revising ("envisioning again").

The author describes loneliness as an ache that can create an urgency we can use to reconnect with the world. By responding to our ache, we can use it to reconnect with the world. By responding to our ache, we can be propelled deeper into our need for expressing our deepest thoughts and feelings.

I find that writing as Natalie Goldberg suggests always releases a wealth of ideas and a flood of words. The quantity constantly surprises me, even if I am writing about such a mundane topic as an apple. Besides the surface of the fruit, associations with such topics as the story of Adam and Eve or my memories of taking an apple to my teacher in primary school surface to yield stories. Over time, I have directed my writing into keeping a journal, creating fiction and non-fiction and developing my book. If you have the slightest urge to write, the delightful free process outlined in *Writing Down The Bones* can help you to know yourself better plus discover and release your creativity. Then you can shape your flow of words into whatever form you wish such as a play, a novel, a story, a poem or entries in a journal.

What We Ache For: Creativity and the Unfolding of Your Soul.

By Oriah Mountain Dreamer.

New York: HarperCollins, 2005.

This book is an invitation to cultivate your creative impulses. Oriah
Mountain Dreamer believes that we must also get in touch with our
spirituality. She defines this as the direct experience of that which is,
paradoxically, the essence of what we are plus that which is larger
than us (i.e., God, the Sacred Mystery or our Higher Power).

In addition, we must feel our sexuality, the beauty and fire of physical existence experienced through our senses. When we allow our
creativity, spirituality and sexuality to flow through us, we can shape
something new, see who we are, know what we value and cultivate
our passion for living with joy.

There are chapters on topics such as beginning to create, learning
to see, contacting our inner silences, taking risks and sacrificing what
does not fit our creation. The author discusses practical and social
areas like as revising, creating together with other writers and taking
our work into the public domain to a gallery or a publisher. At the
end of each chapter, you will find questions for contemplation, interesting suggestions for doing creative work and writing exercises.

Oriah Mountain Dreamer makes us aware of the importance of
focusing upon our intentions plus daring to surrender to surprises.
Whatever path we embrace, she urges us to love the process of creating and to be faithful to the truth we wish to express.

I found this book to be a valuable tool for understanding creativity
and for finding my unique direction. I picked up the book at a time
when I was restless and scattered. I knew that I wanted to create by
writing in addition to drawing and painting. The title seemed to jump
up and embrace my yearning soul. Gradually, I became focused and

returned to writing in my journal, renewing my commitment to finishing this book and adding cartoon illustrations to enhance the text.

A Creative Companion: How to Free Your Creative Spirit.
By SARK.
Berkeley, California: Celestial Arts, 1991.

SARK begins her book with the words "You are invited to be delighted—games, inspirations and surprises." A colorful wreath in brilliant shades of green, purple, pink, orange and yellow surround this invitation. The author fulfills her promise with a unique book. The text is printed by hand in black and colors. The words and letters change from sparkling turquoise to bright orange to intense green to hot pink to deep purple. Charming drawings of people, trees and objects enhance the text.

SARK invites us to experience our world in new creative ways. She suggests having a moonlight picnic or studying something in nature for an hour such as ants or leaves. There are many ideas on how to free our creative spirits. SARK presents tips on how to visualize and relax. One stimulating page describes ways to be really alive
with advice to live juicy, be ridiculous, eat mangoes naked and delight someone. Another page gives us ways to treasure an old person by listening closely, visiting with an awareness of magic and planning something outrageous. Welcoming a new baby and learning how to be an artist are other themes, all presented in glorious colors. The author also describes exercises for relaxing, playing and dreaming and shares her favorite books.

I found this work fun to read, a joy to apply the exercises and a visual delight. It is possible to open it at any page and flow with new experiences, ideas and sensations. Whenever I am feeling a bit blank or blue, just looking at the brilliant colors sparks my creative juices and stimulates me to play, paint, doodle or draw.

Do I Want A Pet?

The Cat and the Curmudgeon.

By Cleveland Amory.

Boston: Little, Brown & Co., 1990.

Polar Bear is the cat and the curmudgeon he owns is Cleveland Amory. Polar Bear became a celebrity after Amory's earlier book *The Cat Who Came for Christmas*, where he told of their initial meeting and early relationship. In this book, the author describes their domestic struggles for power at home and beyond in such places as the park and trips to other states. Amory shares his adventures with Polar Bear as they mingle with other species, meet celebrities and encounter a variety of ladies as he searches for romance for himself.

Cleveland Amory is a writer of great wit and breadth of knowledge. He was a champion of animal rights and the founder of the "Fund for Animals," one of the American anti-cruelty societies.

I experienced a continuous smile and frequent chuckles as I read this book. The author reveals both the ups and downs of living with a feline. As a cat lover, owned by two felines, I easily related to Amory's descriptions of the challenges of living with Polar Bear. Whenever loneliness strikes, I know that I am not totally alone and only have to turn towards my fur babies for a dose of unconditional love. They always respond with purrs of contentment when given strokes or hugs. I quickly forget the times when they chase a ping pong ball along the tile floors in the heart of the night as I try to sleep.

Angel Animals: Exploring Our Spiritual Connection With Animals.

By Allen & Linda Anderson (eds).

New York: Plume, 1999.

If you are considering enriching your life with the love, affection and companionship of a pet, this book will move you to take action. The work is arranged in the following three parts: discovering your spiritual connection with all life, learning how to love unconditionally, and creating family harmony. People describe the profound bond they had with animals; included are a wide range such as dogs, cats, horses, deer and dolphins. They learned lessons about such qualities as courage, loyalty, forgiveness and trust.

The Andersons created an organization called "Angel Animals" in 1996. They conduct workshops for pet owners to deepen the bond between them and their pets. See www.angelanimals.net their website for the *Angel Animals Network*.

Reading this book expanded my awareness of the variety of ways we can help animals of all types. This can give us a feeling of connection with living creatures besides people, so important when we live alone. I know a lady who supports and visits a donkey on a farm. I have other friends who regularly feed squirrels, ducks and birds. Other people in my life send money to humane societies and wildlife organizations or support animals at a zoo.

Chicken Soup for the Pet Lover's Soul: Stories About Pets as Teachers, Healers, Heroes and Friends.

By Marty Becker, Jack Canfield, Carol Kline and Mark Victor Hansen.
Deerfield Beach, Florida: Health Communications, Inc., 1998.

If you have any doubts about living with a companion animal, reading this book is likely to change your mind. People share their stories about the special bonds that they have with animals. The authors tell how animals comfort, inspire, teach and heal them to live richer lives.

I was deeply touched by several tales. A widow tells about when her late husband had a puppy delivered to her on the first Christmas that she faced alone after his death. An anonymous author describes the following things that we can learn from a dog: how to run, romp and play every day, how to enjoy the comfort of constant loyalty, how to delight in the simple joy of a long walk, and how to eat with gusto and enthusiasm. A senior tells how her poodle alerted her to a cancerous lump on her chest in time for successful treament; the dog kept touching and sniffing the area and would throw himself against the diseased spot. A cat named Freddy helped his owner to continue to run her shelter for lost, stray and abandoned animals after someone broke in and killed over 25 cats. Entertaining cartoons and moving quotations are sprinkled throughout the book.

I experienced an appreciation for dogs and cats plus the entire animal kingdom. I was moved by accounts written by people about their bonds with a horse, a gorilla, a mouse or a deer. I shed several tears when I read stories about how people handled the loss of their pets. I was convinced that no home should be without a pet, especially when we live alone.

Seven Cats & the Art of Living.

By Jo Coudert.

New York:Warner Books, 1996.

Jo Coudert, an American writer, shares her experiences with seven cats that had been a part of her life and the lessons she learned from each of them. She presents detailed, sensitive biographies of the felines, intertwined with her observations on how their personalities and behaviors offer wise guidelines for the life of human beings. Some examples are: just be and sit with yourself, develop perseverance, value yourself, give love and kindness to yourself and others, and be yourself. Delightful drawings of the cats will enhance your reading pleasure.

Jo states that "very little in this life is more consoling than a purring body in one's lap and the soft feel of fur under one's hand." As a confirmed cat lover, I definitely agree. I often turn towards my cats for comfort when I am feeling lonely at home alone. My fur babies, Angel and Star, always welcome a massage and teach me lessons on relaxation and unconditional love as they sleep most of the time and get up only for food, the litter, a hug and a bit of exercise.

After reading this book, even if you are not in love with felines, you will certainly look at them with more respect and perhaps even awe. At the end, you will surely agree with the author that one can find meanings and lessons for life from great lives, books, people, nature, stories and cats! You are likely to rush out immediately to acquire a feline to add joy, companionship and warmth to your home if you are not owned by a cat.

Marley & Me: Life and Love with the World's Worst Dog.
By John Grogan.

New York: Morrow, 2005.

John and Jenny adopted Marley, a Labrador retriever, when he was a puppy. As an adult, Marley weighed close to 100 pounds, becoming a boisterous bundle of energy and mischief. Wild and strong, this dog failed at obedience school. He chewed everything in sight, crashed through screen doors and destroyed furniture. Marley constantly drooled copiously. At the same time, he was a devoted pet, offering constant companionship and unconditional love to the author, his wife and children. My heart broke when I read about Marley being put down.

John Grogan, a columnist for the *Philadelphia Inquirer* and past editor-in-chief of *Rodale's Organic Gardening* magazine, writes with great wit at a nippy pace. He emphasizes how Marley taught him to live each day with joy, to appreciate simple things like a walk in the woods and to maintain optimism in the face of adversity as he watched the dog face old age. Most of all, Marley helped John to know about friendship, selflessness and unwavering loyalty.

I laughed and cried as I read about some of the happiest chapters in the author's life with his beloved Marley. As I reflected upon the challenges of coping with Marley's antics, I was deeply moved by the special bond that existed between this dog and his human. The author accepted his beloved canine through all of his mischievous behaviour and illnesses. I know that having an animal companion can be a wonderful blessing as well as a responsibility—yet worth it.

The New Work of Dogs: Tending to Life, Love and Family.
By Jon Katz.
New York: Villard Books, 2003.
Katz tells how dogs are treated as family members in today's world. She describes how they play many roles. These include assisting the blind, helping emotionally disturbed children, comforting people who are lonely or elderly and working in security by protecting property and sniffing for contraband. Long gone are the days when dogs were only hunters.

The book consists of personal stories and sympathetic commentary based on hundreds of interviews with dog owners, breeders, veterinarians, rescuers, trainers and psychiatrists. There are many heart-wrenching tales. One dog was a companion to a man with few human friends. Another dog gave his old owner a reason for living. Dogs of many divorced women helped them to cope with the changes and losses in their lives. A deeply moving chapter tells the stories of people devoted to rescuing dogs in order to prevent their deaths at animal shelters.

Any dog lover will be deeply touched by the stories in this book. I am a fan of felines but now I always look at a dog with respect and reverence. Their loyalty and ability to help people in so many ways makes them remarkable pets. If you are considering a dog to enrich your life alone, this book will help you to be certain about your decision to choose one as your pet.

Shall I Seek a Partner......or Not?

Finding True Love: The Four Essential Keys to Discovering the Love of Your Life.

By Daphne Rose Kingma.

Berkeley, CA: Conari Press, 1996.

Do you crave a close, intimate relationship? Do you want comfort, passion and companionship with a significant other? Even though I love my cats, my home and most aspects of my life, I still sometimes yearn for a man to share my journey on a regular basis.

I seek guidance from this book each time before I hunt for Mr. Right. Kingma is a therapist who writes eloquently and compassionately. She presents an enlightening look at the inner work we can do to attract a deep love, focusing upon spiritual and emotional preparations.

One key is faith, believing that the true love that you desire is there for you. While waiting, you can be open to meet new people, fix your home and take actions such as replying to ads.

Another key is intention—to deeply want a loving relationship in your heart and soul. You can prepare yourself by pursuing self-knowledge, knowing what you are looking for and what you have to offer, plus being aware of your lifestyle. The author suggests asking yourself the following questions. How do you want to be loved? Why has love eluded you? Kingma stresses that as we become more loving, we are likely to attract love. It is important to cultivate qualities like appreciation, generosity and kindness.

As I prepare for that special person, this book offers a fascinating range of ideas for inner work that I can do to make me more loveable. After reading about the keys to finding true love, I can accept and honour where I am and embrace myself (as well as my cats), seeing myself as a deserving lover. At the end of the book, there is a "Love Readiness Inventory" to answer the question, "Is this the One for Me?," to help to guide me with the leap into the dating scene.

Celibacy Is Better Than Really Bad Sex: And Other Classic Rules For Single Women.

By Patti Putnicki.

Los Angeles: Corkscrew Press, 1994.

Patti Putnicki, 35 years of age, a single white female from Dallas Texas at the time of writing this book, begins by telling us to think of dating as continuing education. We are advised to keep our sense of humour and hold on to our self-esteem in order to maintain our sanity. The author emphasizes that we can have fun in the dating game as long as we focus upon the humorous aspects of our experiences.

The book consists of 26 rules to guide a single lady facing the dating scene. For example, Rule Number 4 is "If He Says His Wife Doesn't Understand Him, Suggest He Enroll in Berlitz." Rule Number 21 is "If He Says He Needs Space, Suggest He Move to Utah." Rule Number 24 gives advice about coping when Mr. Wrong wants to hitch you and Mr. Right wants to ditch you. There are delightful illustrations that enhance her description of the rules. The text is creatively presented with spaces in between the messages, the use of headings and sub-headings, numbered lists and bullets. So, the book is easy and fun to read.

Putnicki's rules confirm my decision to choose, accept and even enjoy celibacy at times rather than leaping into an undesirable relationship. I consult the book before, during and after ventures into the dating scene in order to keep looking at the brighter and lighter side of mingling with the opposite sex.

Even God is Single: (so stop giving me a hard time).

By Karen Salmansohn. (Illustrated by Ed Fortheringham).
New York, Workman Publishing Company, 2000.

Delightful cartoons in red, black and white plus brief captions address the question, "Why aren't you married?" Salmansohn offers this book to single gals to remind us to feel good about singlehood and presents feisty replies to this question.

She points out that even Hitler and Frankenstein got married. Yet, Catwoman, Buddha and God remained single. The author stresses that there is no need to rush into marriage by a certain age when one can lie about one's age. We have the freedom to hold out for a spouse who is more than a walking wallet. The best things in life are free such as free love, being yeast infection-free and "toilet seat un-free." Both married and single people have problems, so it is a matter of deciding which kind of problems we want to have.

This book gives me many chuckles. I follow Salmansohn's advice to focus upon becoming more communicative, soulful, honest and sexually talented. Then, I can be a better person and a happier marital partner when and if I choose this path.

Online Dating For Dummies.

By Judith Silverstein and Michael Lasky.
Hoboken, N.J.:Wiley Publishing, Inc., 2004.
The authors met through online dating and established a long distance romantic relationship. They interviewed thousands of daters and studied hundreds of online sites for this book. Silverstein and Lasky recommend online dating since it offers such features as convenience, a limitless supply of people and the opportunity to e-mail many people simultaneously in order to choose appropriate matches.

Silverstein and Lasky discuss every aspect of using the internet to find a partner. Besides information on hardware and software for the novice, there is material on acronyms such as LOL for laugh out loud and emoticons, keyboard created faces and instant messaging procedures. In-depth chapters are full of practical tips for selecting a photograph for your profile, choosing screen names and first lines, answering open-ended questions, sending and replying to initial e-mails and answering open-ended questions. There are also valuable chapters on safety when going from virtual to real contact, handling rejection and detecting frauds, players and even criminals. Finally, there are suggestions for selecting a dating service and reviews of common sites like Lavalife and Yahoo.com personals.

After consulting this book, I have gone surfing many times seeking the love of my life. Alas! Online matchmaking services have yielded me dates but I have not yet met Mr. Right. I have dated several widowers who were still grieving the loss of their wives after many years, footloose and fancy-free divorced men and single men who are not looking for a commitment. However, the book has given me many great tips for revising my profile and suggestions for ways of sending and replying to e-mails.

The Joy of NOT Being Married: The Essential Guide for Singles (And Those Who Wish They Were).
By Ernie Zelinski.
Edmonton, Alberta: Visions International Publishing, 1995.
Zelinski writes about how to be a happy single person and live life to the fullest. He suggests several directions to pursue. First of all, it is important to have a purpose, a personal mission where we respond with passion; it can be expressed through areas like our work, our hobbies and our volunteer work. Second, we must develop a sense of community with supportive relationships. Third, we have to celebrate being alone. As we cherish our solitude, we can learn and grow and cultivate a strong sense of ourselves, knowing our needs, desires and values. Fourth, it is important to have self-esteem, to like and enjoy our own company by pursuing meaningful activities. Have a love affair with yourself and treat yourself as you would a best friend or ideal lover.

Yes, time, effort, courage and perseverance are required. Yet, the rewards are plentiful. Living alone means that we can enjoy our freedom, mobility, adventures, and opportunities for creativity. Thus, we can feel deeply alive and full of a zest for life. Zelinski cautions against having the TV, fridge and couch as our three best friends. Rather, we can pursue our interests at leisure to involve ourselves with whatever turns us on.

The author also discusses aspects of a successful and realistic romantic relationship and presents tips for meeting partners. However, Zelinski stresses that marriage does not lead to Nirvana. He suggests that when we get over our need to be attached and stop defining ourselves in terms of a relationship, we can experience deep contentment. If Mr. or Ms. Right shows up, that will be great; if not, that's okay too.

Ernie Zelinski is a single man who writes in a warm friendly style, drawing upon his own life and works by many authors. A most delightful and useful feature of the book is his use of signs throughout the work, labelled "Your Singles Advantage." There are captions such as: "you can stay up as long as you want; you can sleep diagonally on a king-sized bed" and "you have more clothes closet space." I made a list of most of his words of wisdom and consult it frequently. I smile and feel great about being single and count my blessings after I read this book.

101 More Reasons Why A Cat is Better than a Man.

By Allia Zobel. Illustrations by Nicole Hollander.
Holbrook, Mass.: Adams Media, 1997.

An author and illustrator present hilarious pearls of wisdom and delightful coloured cartoons for the feline fancier who is owned by a cat. Here are samples of the sayings, bound to tickle your funny bone. "Cats figure if you gain a few pounds, so what? There's more of you to love. Cats are never late for dinner. Cats put you on a pedestal. Cats always find you exciting—no matter how many years you've been together. A cat would never suggest a trial separation. A cat will follow you anywhere. But he'll never lead you on." The book is compact (five inches by five inches) and easily fits into a pocket or purse.

Whenever I read this book, I wonder why I would ever prefer a man to a cat. I ponder the last thought expressed in the book. "A cat will love you forever." I think about the men who have come and gone in my life and burst with gratitude for my loyal felines, Angel and Star.

I must conclude, however, that cats and men are different, cats being better in some ways and worse in others. Cats constantly offer unconditional love. Yet, although you can drive your cat to the veterinarian at times of sickness, he or she cannot return the favour and take you to the doctor when you are ill. A man might not be as steady in his affection for you. But, he can drive you places, take you out for dinner, engage in two-way verbal communication and offer sexual pleasure. So, the ideal situation is to have both a cat and a man in your life.

LaVergne, TN USA
26 January 2010

171114LV00001B/25/P